HOW TO DOUBLE
YOUR TAX REFUND

A Simple Guide to
Managing Your Taxes and Getting Free Money

Daniel J. Pilla

WINNING Publications, Inc.
St. Paul, Minnesota

WINNING Publications, Inc.
2372 Leibel Street
White Bear Lake, MN 55110
www.taxhelponline.com

First Edition, June, 1999

Printed in the United States of America

ISBN: 1-884367-04-6

Notice from the Author and Publisher

This book is designed to provide the author's findings and
opinions based on research, analysis and experience with the subject
matter covered. This information is not provided for purposes of
rendering legal, accounting or other professional advice. It is
intended purely for educational purposes.

The author and the publisher disclaim any responsibility for
any liability or loss incurred as a consequence of the use and
application, either directly or indirectly of any information presented
herein.

Because the United States currently operates under an
evolutionary legal system, the reader bears the burden of assuring
that the principles of law stated in this work are current and binding
at the time of any intended use or application.

Caution: The law in this country is subject to change arbitrarily and
without prior notice.

Dedication

To Jeannie . . .

Then the LORD God made a woman from the
rib he had taken out of the man, and he brought her to
the man.

The man said, "This is now bone of my bones and flesh
of my flesh; she shall be called 'woman,' for she was
taken out of man."

For this reason a man will leave his father
and mother and be united to his wife, and they will
become one flesh.

Genesis 2:22-24

TABLE OF CONTENTS

TABLE OF ABBREVIATIONS

DIF--Discriminate Function System
EITC--Earned Income Tax Credit
FSA--Flexible Spending Arrangement
IC--Independent Contractor
IRA--Individual Retirement Account
IRC--Internal Revenue Code
IRM--Internal Revenue Manual
IRP--Information Returns Program
IRS--Internal Revenue Service
MSA--Medical Savings Account
REV. PROC.--Revenue Procedure
REV. REG.--Revenue Regulation
REV. RUL.--Revenue Ruling
SEP--Simplified Employee Pension
SIMPLE--Savings Inventive Match Plan for
    Employees
TA--Taxpayer Advocate
TC MEMO--Tax Court Memorandum court
    decision

About the Author . . .

For over two decades, Dan Pilla has been tremendously successful in his negotiations with the IRS. Nationally regarded as an expert in IRS procedures, Dan provides people like you with sound solutions to their tax problems. Dan's proven techniques effectively manage and resolve tax problems of every kind.

As one of the nation's first and leading defenders of taxpayer rights, Dan has defended nearly every kind of deduction. In a previous book entitled, *Smart Taxes*, Dan guaranteed an extra $1,000 in tax deductions. In his latest release, *How to Double Your Tax Refund*, Dan makes another guarantee--that your tax refund *will* double if you follow the simple procedures Dan outlines.

Dan has presented testimony to Congress on several issues relating to taxpayers' rights, tax policy and administration. His 1996 release, *IRS, Taxes and the Beast* blew the lid off IRS abuse and provided the foundation for the Senate Finance Committee's hearings into IRS abuse. Many of Dan's suggestions for IRS reforms were incorporated into the Internal Revenue Service Restructuring Act.

Dan's work has been recognized by the likes of CNN, CBS, CNBC, Fox Network News and the USA Radio Network. His books have been recommended by leading magazines and financial journals such as *Money Magazine*, *Family Circle*, *Wall Street Journal*, *Investors Business Daily* and many others. Dan was a tax policy consultant to four presidential candidates and was an official consultant to the National Commission on Restructuring the IRS, the US Taxpayer's Party, the National Taxpayer's Union and many other taxpayers' groups.

INTRODUCTION

In 1999, the average American paid a greater percentage of his income in taxes than at any other time in our history. In fact, the average family now pays more in taxes than it does in food, clothing, shelter and medical care--combined. Each year on April 15, the Tax Foundation, a non-partisan public policy research institute in Washington, D.C., releases its Tax Freedom Day calculation. This is the day of the year on which a person would have earned enough money to pay all his taxes--federal state and local--if every dollar earned beginning January 1 of the year was committed to taxes. In 1999, Tax Freedom Day fell on May 11, one day later than the previous high-water mark of May 10, set in 1998.

The growing tax burden puts a substantial squeeze on the budgets of low and middle income families. The average family in the 1990s faces a total tax burden of about 40-45 percent of income. In 1996, the median family income for a dual income family was $53,091. That family paid a total of $21,883 for federal, state and local taxes. To see why the average middle income family today cannot survive on a single income, we need only examine the tax burden faced by families of the 1950s, when most lived comfortably with larger families, one income and a stay-at-home mom.

In 1955, the average family paid (in 1996 inflation-adjusted dollars) just $6,665 in taxes at all levels. Today's family pays more than three times what our parents did on the same relative income. Throughout the decades of the 1950s and '60s, the total tax burden for the average family never exceeded 22 to

25 percent of income. Today, the burden is as high as 45 percent. No wonder life is a struggle for so many families.

From 1993 to 1999, the average family's total tax burden has grown dramatically. In 1993, for example, Tax Freedom Day fell on April 30. In 1999, it falls well into the second week of May. Tax policy has stolen nearly two more weeks of your working life in just seven short years. The question that looms largely is, "How has government been able to raise taxes so much?"

While there are many reasons, the most compelling is that most Americans simply do not realize how much they pay in taxes. For most Americans, their tax burden is well hidden. Hidden taxes allow the government to raise rates without the citizens detecting who is to blame.

At present, nearly 85 percent of Americans do not "pay" taxes per se. Instead, their taxes are *withheld* from their paychecks and sent to the government by their employers. This is a system known as wage withholding, a product of the Victory Tax Act of 1943, a "temporary" measure put into the law while America was at war.

Since then, wage withholding has expanded substantially. It now covers not only federal income taxes but social security taxes as well. In addition, state income taxes are likewise withheld from our weekly pay and forwarded to the various state agencies that administer them. The system is so efficient that most people actually end up overpaying their taxes, which leads to the annual ritual of getting a tax refund.

The unholy combination of wage withholding and a tax refund has more than a few people convinced they do not pay taxes at all. In my work as a Tax Litigation Consultant helping people solve tax collection and other related IRS problems, I often ask a client, "How much did you pay in taxes last year?" It is not at all unusual for the client to respond by saying, "I didn't pay anything. I got a refund." The conversation goes something like this:

"Is that so?" I ask. "How much was your refund?" The client answers by saying, "$1,000."

"That's good," I say. "Let's look at your W-2 Form."

The Form W-2, *Wage and Tax Statement*, is a form prepared by the employer at the end of the year. It reports to both the employee and the IRS total wages paid and the amount of withholding from wages on account of both federal and state income taxes and social security taxes.

After examining the W-2, I say, "This W-2 Form shows that you had about $5,000 in wage withholding. And you say you received a $1,000 refund. Now let me ask you again--how much did you pay in taxes last year?"

Presented with these facts, the client quickly realizes that he in fact paid $4,000 in taxes. But because the tax was both hidden in wage withholding and covered by the refund, he believed he did not pay anything. Much to his own embarrassment, he discovered that he indeed is a taxpayer--in a big way.

Of course, this illustration does not even take into account the social security tax. Nobody receives a refund of social security taxes nor do they prepare a social security tax return or make separate payments of social security taxes. As such, the social security tax is totally hidden. Consequently, people have no idea that they pay more in social security taxes-- even at half the rate of the lowest income tax bracket--than they do in federal income taxes. To be sure, the idea of a hidden tax has served the architects of our high tax government quite well but at great expense to the American family.

This brings us to the issue of the income tax refund--the topic of this book. Each year, tens of millions of citizens anxiously await their federal and state income tax refunds. In 1999, approximately 88.76 million citizens got tax refunds totaling $139.46 billion, or an average of over $1,570 per refund. This is a 14 percent increase over the 1998 average refund, which was $1,335. Each spring, citizens drop their returns in the mail impatiently awaiting what they consider to be a gift from the government. What they get in reality is a small fraction of what they paid during the previous year but lost track of due to government-designed accounting sleight of hand.

In addition to losing sight of the total amount they paid during the course of the year, too many people also lose sight of the reason they get the refund in the first place. A tax refund is not a gift from the government; it is a return of the money *you* overpaid. In order to get a refund, you must have first paid too much in taxes. And if you paid too much in taxes, that means you deprived yourself and your family of money you could have saved, invested or spent on necessary living expenses.

The worst part of this is the government held your money for well over a year and did not pay you one dime of interest. In this way, American families are deprived of over $6.97 billion in capital growth they otherwise might have realized had the money been available for normal investment or savings purposes during the course of the year.

Based upon the lost interest alone, I am sure you will agree that allowing the IRS to keep your money for over a year is not a good idea. But our challenge here is not just to even the odds in the refund game; our goal is to turn the tables in the refund game. Rather than live life in the hope of an average $1,570 refund, why not double--even triple--your refund? Yes, it can be done and it can be done using the simple, easy to understand strategies discussed in this book.

To get yourself on the road to accomplishing this goal, you must be willing take some initiative to better your financial condition. Are you willing to take steps to do that? Begin by answering this question: "Is IRS better suited to manage your money for the benefit of you and your family than you are?" If you said "no," then you are ready to begin your journey.

Let us start with a harsh fact of life. That fact is, *taxes make you poorer*. Every dollar you pay in taxes means there is one less dollar available to provide food for your family. Every dollar you pay in taxes means there is one less dollar available to pay for your family's heath care. Every dollar you pay in taxes means there is one less dollar available to save for your retirement. Every dollar you pay in taxes means there is one less dollar available to invest in a business opportunity for the future. Every dollar you pay in taxes means there is one less dollar available to pay existing debt, such as a home mortgage or credit cards. Every dollar you pay in taxes means there is one less dollar available to pay for your children's education.

Taxes make you poorer. This is best illustrated with another comparison between tax rates of the 1950s and '60s and those of today. If the overall tax burden of the low 20 percent range present during the 1950s and '60s was maintained throughout the decades of the 1980s and '90s, our country's gross national product would be about double what it is now. The impact of this on the average family is staggering. It means that today, families would have about twice as much real income and about $100,000 more in assets owned outright--*free of debt*--as they have now.

Which would you rather have: high taxes or double your current annual income? Which would you rather have: high taxes or $100,000 more cash in the bank or equity in your home? I rather suspect you would opt for the latter. That being the situation, you must be willing to take control of your tax life to optimize the opportunities available to you.

By successfully following the procedures in this book, you can increase your personal wealth substantially without increasing your gross pay. It is like getting a tax-free pay raise. By putting your refund to work for you properly, you can expect to double or even triple its real value. The old adage saying that a penny saved is a penny earned is amplified by about 100 percent when it comes to taxes. In reality, a dollar saved in taxes is like two dollars of income earned. Most of us do not have the ability to simply double our incomes overnight but we certainly can double our refunds with a few simple steps. In addition, you can look forward to an immediate increase in your take-home pay, tax-free returns on your investments and much more, as you will learn later.

Many investment advisors tell us that the largest expenditure you will make in your lifetime is your home. Therefore, advisors counsel you to take great care when making the investment. Consider the real estate tax liability incident to ownership. Consider the out-of-pocket costs to maintain the home. Consider the location and potential for future appreciation, etc.

Certainly, this advice is sound. However, the initial premise is *not* true. Your single largest lifetime expenditure is not your home--not by a long shot. By far and away, the single largest expense you incur is taxes. Regardless of the amount of your monthly house payment, at some point the note is paid off.

Considering just minimal increases in value, the majority of what you put into the house (if not more) will generally be there in the form of equity in later years. With taxes, on the other hand, no matter how much you pay, you *never* have equity in *anything*.

The conclusion should be obvious. You must begin to approach your tax situation with at least as much forethought, care and consideration as you do home ownership. In your attempt to manage your household budget, you must pay more attention to managing your tax liability than you do any other expense. You might just be surprised at what it can mean in terms of return on the time invested.

-- Daniel J. Pilla

CHAPTER ONE
The Cost of Overpaying Your Taxes

All economic resources are finite. This is especially true for middle-income Americans. Every family must make financial choices on a regular basis. The choices involve deciding whether to purchase a new car this year or fix the present car and wait another year. Do we take a family vacation this summer or add a screen porch to the house? For too many families, the questions are as fundamental as whether or not to buy new clothing for the children. The list of possible questions is endless and I know of no family that does not engage in this kind of discourse.

Because our financial resources are limited, we must be good stewards over those we have. We cannot squander our money. Since most of us have limited earning potential, it is very difficult to make up that which is lost. This attitude makes most middle-income Americans conservative when it comes to their money. That conservative nature renders people quite unwilling to take risks. And while it is generally good to avoid risk--especially unnecessary risk--often that unwillingness leads to another kind of cost--that cost associated with lost opportunity.

Those unwilling to break out and explore beyond their immediate sphere of life often miss out on a great many things. This is especially true in the financial arena. Admittedly, however, most middle-income families cannot venture into the area of high finance because they do not have the capital resources available to put at risk. A growing number of middle-income Americans struggle just to make ends meet on a monthly basis. Some even live paycheck to paycheck, without much hope of building a nest egg.

In too many cases, our personal attitude about taxes makes matters worse. For those Americans who get a tax refund each year, not only are they giving up the use of the money for more than one year but they lose the potential increase on that money as well. This is a lost opportunity and comes at a very high cost in most cases.

In addition to allowing the IRS to keep more than is owed, most Americans just overpay their taxes outright. By that I mean they do not claim all the tax breaks and deductions the law allows. In my experience of more than two decades as a tax professional, I find that the vast majority of Americans opt not to claim the deductions they are entitled to rather than risk a potential audit. In other words, people believe that by not claiming deductions, they have somehow purchased some measure of protection. Ironically, this approach does not prevent an audit. All it does is ensure that you pay more than you legally owe. It also ensures that you have fewer precious financial resources available to provide your family's needs or increase its standard of living.

This is surely one key reason why so few people can save money today. Nearly one-third of all families live paycheck to paycheck. In the last fifteen years, consumer debt--driven largely by credit card borrowing--has increased more than 350 percent. In the last five years, more Americans have borrowed against their home equity than at any other time in our history. In 1997 and 1998 respectively, records were set, then broken on the number of consumer bankruptcies filed. Whereas during the early and mid 1990s our national savings rate languished at an anemic 2 percent, in February, 1999, for the first time in history, it dropped below zero.

It seems Americans cannot save money. And the overriding reason can be expressed in one word--taxes. Under the best of cases, taxes consume more of the family budget than food, clothing, shelter and medical care combined. Under the worst of cases, taxes put a person into the position of having to make a choice between paying them or feeding the family. What is even worse is people *voluntarily* exacerbate the situation by allowing the IRS to hold their money interest-free and by willingly paying more than they owe, though clearly, they cannot afford to. Overpaying taxes robs your family of the resources it needs to survive and prosper. The most important obligation you have is to provide for your family. That is your first duty and it should be paramount in all your deliberations.

To better understand what really happens when you allow the IRS to keep your money, I shall illustrate with a common example. Suppose you receive the average refund, which, in 1999, was $1,570. In order to get that refund, you must overpay your taxes. Specifically, you pay $130 per month in taxes you do not owe. Furthermore, you do not get your refund on January 1 of the following year. You cannot get the refund until you file your return. If you file in March, as many people do, you get your refund in May--maybe later. By the time you get your $1,570 refund, you have undergone four to five additional months of withholding. The IRS now has at least $520 more to apply to the new year--maybe more.

As a result of the withholding for the current year, your $1,570 refund is not worth $1,570. Because of the $520 worth of new withholding, the $1,570 refund is really worth $1,050. Even if you file your return electronically, you cannot avoid at least two to four months of additional withholding to cover the new year. Because of this, you never break even with the IRS. The agency *always* owes you money.

If you did nothing more than reduce your withholding to match your tax liability, then took the additional $130 per month and simply stashed it in a mattress you would be ahead of the game. Consider the facts. Your refund is really worth $1,050 by the time you receive it. However, by eliminating over-withholding, you get an extra $130 per month in after-tax take home pay. As such, you have $1,570 in real money by January 1 of the following year. Moreover, you also have the $520 you saved between January and April when you would otherwise receive the refund. The simple act of eliminating the over-withholding increases the real value of your refund from $1,050 to $2,090, or about 200 percent. This does not even take into account the cost of the lost opportunity--the inability to invest and grow the money the IRS holds. This is documented later with greater clarity.

This example only begins to illustrate the cost of over-withholding. As we progress through this treatise, you will learn many other ways to put your money to work for you, giving you additional tax advantages and helping you save that which you worked too hard to acquire.

The above example of how costly over-withholding is begs the question, why do so many people do it? In answering this question, we begin to dispel the myths that lead to over-withholding. In turn, we can begin to set people and their money free to work and grow--as they should. There are three primary reasons why people allow over-withholding to continue. I address each one in turn.

1. Misunderstanding the Form W-4. Form W-4, *Employee's Withholding Allowance Certificate*, is one of the most misunderstood IRS forms. Most people do not understand the full purpose of the form nor do they understand how to complete it. Just as bad, most people file the form once when they begin a job, then never look at it again. This could be the chief reason why so many people over-withhold.

In the chapters immediately following this discussion, we examine the W-4 in detail and explain the things you need to know to complete one correctly and in a manner that does not lead to over-withholding. The W-4 is an important tool in the battle to turn the tide against high taxes. When you finish with these next several chapters, you will understand exactly what you can and cannot do vis-à-vis the W-4.

2. The savings account. Many people treat the income tax withholding system as a kind of savings account. They deliberately over-withhold so the IRS acts like a bank, holding their money so they do not spend it. As shown above, however, this is the *world's worst* way to save money. Not only do you never break even with the IRS but the IRS pays you no interest and you cannot use the money to better your financial condition. You are doing yourself no favor by "saving" money in this fashion.

Many respond by saying this is the only way they can discipline themselves to actually save the money. If they got an extra $130 each month they would just spend it. Okay. But what do you do with the $1,570 refund when you receive it? Do you save it? Do you invest it someplace? Or do you splurge once a year? A vacation, a new stereo, a new...?

If you allow the government to hold your money interest-free for up to sixteen months only to blow it when you get your refund, maybe over-withholding is a way to have money to binge. But if you *really* want to save money, if you *really* are trying to find a way to increase your net worth, reduce debt and save taxes, over-withholding is--I repeat--*the world's worst way to do it!*

At the very least, put $130 per month into a savings account. Even getting a lousy 3 percent interest is better than lending it to the government interest-free, especially if you are just going to blow it at the end of the year. At least this way, the money is available in December to buy Christmas gifts and you get the benefit of the interest.

But there are many far superior and faster ways to save money. In later chapters of this book, we explore several ideas on how to use the $130 per month to build your financial nest egg in ways that do not tempt you to spend the money.

3. *Fear of the IRS.* At every level, fear of the IRS immobilizes people. There can be no doubt that fear plays a role in over-withholding income taxes as well. In fact, as discussed earlier, fear drives many to over-pay on the off chance that it might buy them some protection from an audit. Likewise, nobody wants to face the staggering interest and penalties assessed by the IRS for underpaying taxes. We all know those penalties can be crippling.

But the potential of interest and penalties should not be allowed to stand in the way of better financial conditions for you and your family. In the first place, penalties and interest only apply when you deliberately disregard the tax laws and regulations. They do not apply, as we examine later, to those who make honest mistakes in a good faith attempt to comply with the law.

More importantly, the law *does not require* one to pay more taxes than he owes. Consequently, you cannot legally be penalized for adjusting your withholding to match your tax obligation. In all cases, the risk of penalties can be fully managed and completely avoided when handled properly. That, of course, is another of the topics addressed in later chapters.

In summary, it is time to stop wasting the scarce financial resources that have been entrusted to you. It is time to use the basic legal tools available to all of us to begin to multiply those resources for the betterment of you and your family.

CHAPTER TWO
Give Yourself a Pay Raise Today
By Understanding the W-4

To benefit from the system, you must understand the system. While the income tax withholding system is responsible for a great deal of confusion and overpayment of taxes, it is really quite simple. After reading this chapter, you will understand how to make the system work for you instead of the IRS. Once you know how the system really operates, you will be able to give yourself a tax-free pay raise today!

Why Wage Withholding?

Since 1943, when the Victory Tax Act was put into effect, our income tax system has been considered a "pay as you go" system. Courts interpret this to mean that you have an obligation to pay the tax as the income is earned. Even though an official debt for taxes--known as an assessment--is not created until you file your income tax return at the close of the year, your taxes must be paid through sufficient estimated payments during the course of the year. Employees make estimated payments through periodic wage withholding. Self-employed persons make estimated payments directly to the IRS on a quarterly basis.

Most people do not realize, however, that they have personal control over their withholding and estimated payments. Too many wrongfully believe they are completely subject to the IRS' whim in this regard. Such is simply not the case. Wage-earners have the right to control withholding through Form W-4,

Employee's Withholding Allowance Certificate. Self-employed persons have even more control through the vehicle of quarterly estimated payments.

Let us examine the basics of estimated tax payment requirements.

The Amount of Estimated Payments

Internal Revenue Code (the code) section 6654 provides a penalty for failure to make sufficient estimated payments. This is one of the most frequently assessed penalties in the code. The reason is because as a growing number of citizens find themselves unable to pay what they owe, the IRS is quick to assess the full range of penalties at its disposal. Even those who can pay on time are often fearful of penalty assessments. As pointed out in chapter one, this is a key reason why so many people over-withhold, allowing the IRS to use their money indefinitely--free of charge. However, the law *does not* require one to pay more than he owes.

The rules are found in code section 6654(d). It provides that to avoid a penalty for failure to make sufficient estimated payments, one must pay an amount equal to, a) 90 percent of the current year's income tax liability, or b) 100 percent of the prior year's tax liability, whichever is less. To illustrate, suppose you are figuring your estimated payments for 1999. In that case, the current year is 1999 and the prior year is 1998. Suppose further that your total 1998 income tax liability, before withholding credits, was $6,000. Further suppose that your financial circumstances have not changed in any significant way.

Based on these facts, you avoid the penalty if your 1999 estimated payments are at least $5,400. That amount is 90 percent of the $6,000 total tax liability, which is what you will likely owe in 1999. If, however, your income jumps and you anticipate owing $7,000 in 1999 taxes, estimated payments of $6,000 are sufficient to avoid the penalty since that amount is 100 percent of the 1998 total liability.

The rules change slightly for so-called "high income" persons. For those with adjusted gross income of $150,000 or more ($75,000 for married filing separately), the requirement is to pay 90 percent of the current year's liability or 105 percent of the prior year's liability. Code section 6654(d)(1).

In *no case* does the law require one to pay more than he owes in the *current* year. Even in the case of high income citizens, the requirement of estimated payments to be at least 105 percent of the liability applies to the *prior* year's tax, not the current tax. Suppose a high-income citizen had a $20,000 tax debt in 1998 and anticipates no additional income in 1999. Estimated payments of $18,000 (90 percent of the anticipated 1999 liability) are sufficient to avoid the penalty for failure to make sufficient estimated payments.

Figuring Estimated Payments

The primary reason the average person subjects himself to over-withholding is because of his lack of understanding of the Form W-4. Form W-4 is used to communicate to your employer the number of "allowances" you claim for purposes of computing wage withholding. Using IRS Publication 15, *Circular E, Employer's Tax Guide*, your employer takes the number of allowances claimed on your W-4 and your marital status, then refers to a chart showing various weekly or monthly income amounts. From the chart, he determines the withholding necessary based upon those parameters. The fewer the allowances, the more the withholding. The greater the allowances, the less the withholding. It is that simple. Should an employee fail to submit a W-4 to the employer, IRS regulations require the employer to withhold from that person as though he is single with zero allowances.

This is known as the wage bracket method of withholding. It works in situations where there are no more than ten withholding allowances claimed on Form W-4. In cases where more than ten are claimed, one must use the percentage method, which is explained below.

Under code section 3402(f), you are entitled to one allowance for each dependent claimed on your tax return. For tax return purposes, dependents are referred to as exemptions. They include yourself, your spouse and each child or other person the support for whom you pay at least 51 percent during the year. Thus, a married person with three children is entitled to claim five allowances. However, too many people unfairly limit the number of allowances they claim. Many believe you are entitled to claim only your exemptions but no more. This is not true.

Code section 3402(m) provides for additional withholding allowances to account for other items that reduce your tax liability. Allowances can be claimed for both "estimated itemized deductions" (section 3402(m)(1)) and "estimated tax credits" (section 3402(m)(2)) or and other tax return claims that lower your taxes (section 3402(m)(3)). These include loss carry-forwards, capital losses, net operating losses, etc. Internal Revenue Regulation section 31.3402(m)-1 lists the following items that may be included in the calculation of withholding allowances:

(1) All estimated itemized deductions allowable under chapter 1 of the code;

(2) All estimated tax credits allowable under the code except;

    a. the credit for tax withheld on wages;

    b. the credit for tax withheld at source on nonresident aliens and foreign corporations and on tax-free covenant bonds;

    c. the credit for certain uses of gasoline and special fuels but only to the extent that you have not filed for a quarterly tax refund of the credit on Form 843;

    d. the credit for earned income but only to the extent the employee has not filed for advance payments of the credit on Form W-5; and

    e. the credit for overpayment of tax under code section 45;

(3) The estimated unreimbursed trade and business deductions of employees described in code section 62;

(4) The estimated deduction for payments to pension, profit-sharing, annuity and bond purchase plans of self-employed individuals described in section 62 and allowed by code sections 404 and 405(c);

(5) The estimated deduction for penalties forfeited because of premature withdrawal of funds from time savings

accounts or deposits described in code section 62(12) and allowed by code section 165;

(6) The estimated direct charitable deduction under code section 170(i);

(7) The estimated deduction for net operating loss carryovers under code section 172;

(8) The estimated deduction for alimony, etc., payments under code section 215;

(9) The estimated deduction for moving expenses under code section 217 but only to the extent that such amount is not excluded from wages by code section 3401(a)(15);

(10) The estimated deduction for certain retirement savings under code section 219 but only to the extent that such amount is not excluded from wages by code section 3401(a)(12)(D);

(11) The estimated deduction for two-earner married couples under code section 221; and

(12) The estimated net losses from schedules C, *Profit or (Loss) From Business or Profession*, D, *Capital Gains and Losses*, E, *Supplemental Income Schedule*, and F, *Farm Income and Expenses* of Form 1040 and from the last line of Part II of Form 4797, *Supplemental Schedule of Gains and Losses*.

The idea behind the allowance rule is to allow you to adjust your withholding to match your tax liability. You do not want to under-withhold because that leads to a tax bill and potential penalty. You do not want to over-withhold because that gives the government the free use of your money. Therefore, to eliminate over-withholding, simply increase the number of allowances. This is how it works:

First, determine the number of exemptions you may claim. You are allowed one exemption for each dependent claimed on your return. Include any special exemptions, such as that for being over age 65 or legally blind. You may also claim one additional allowance if you are entitled to head of household filing status and you may claim one if you have at least $1,500 of childcare expenses for which you will claim a credit. Suppose that for purposes of illustration, the total number is 5.

Next, calculate the total amount of itemized deductions, tax credits, etc., you expect to claim on your return. Include all items on Schedule A, *Itemized Deductions*. Include tax credits such as the earned income tax credit or the new child credit. Do not forget to include items such as business losses (but not business operating expenses) and capital losses. A simple example illustrates the point. Suppose you have the following:

a. $4,000 charitable contributions;
b. $5,000 mortgage interest;
c. $1,500 real estate taxes;
d. $ 300 miscellaneous;
e. $3,000 capital loss carry-forward;
f. $1,200 child credit;
g. $2,000 IRA contribution.

The total of these items, all of which act to reduce your tax bill, is $17,000. To figure the number of allowances these entitle you to claim, divide the total by $3,000, which is the value of one allowance. The quotient is 5.66. To begin with, round down to the next whole number or in this case, 5.

CAUTION: Allowances are equal in value to exemptions. Therefore, as the exemption amount increases each year, so does the allowance value. You must re-calculate your allowances each year based upon current values and your financial circumstances.

Next, add the number of exemptions (5) and allowances (5), to get the total number of allowances to claim on Form W-4. In this case, the number is 10. For help with this process, please see the worksheet provided with IRS Form W-4. An examination copy is reproduced on the next two pages.

Fine Tuning Your Withholding

In the above example, ten withholding allowances should get you to the point of paying all taxes without excessive withholding. If you have not done this exercise to determine the correct number of allowances, by all means, do so. To refine your withholding, I have worked out a couple of exercises which will fine tune the withholding based upon all the facts and circumstances of your case. Use these exercises if you currently

Form W-4 (1999)

Purpose. Complete Form W-4 so your employer can withhold the correct Federal income tax from your pay. Because your tax situation may change, you may want to refigure your withholding each year.

Exemption from withholding. If you are exempt, complete only lines 1, 2, 3, 4, and 7, and sign the form to validate it. Your exemption for 1999 expires February 16, 2000.

Note: *You cannot claim exemption from withholding if (1) your income exceeds $700 and includes more than $250 of unearned income (e.g., interest and dividends) and (2) another person can claim you as a dependent on their tax return.*

Basic Instructions. If you are not exempt, complete the Personal Allowances Worksheet. The worksheets

on page 2 adjust your withholding allowances based on itemized deductions, adjustments to income, or two-earner/two-job situations. Complete all worksheets that apply. They will help you figure the number of withholding allowances you are entitled to claim. **However, you may claim fewer allowances.**

Child tax and higher education credits. For details on adjusting withholding for these and other credits, see **Pub. 919,** Is My Withholding Correct for 1999?

Head of household. Generally, you may claim head of household filing status on your tax return only if you are unmarried and pay more than 50% of the costs of keeping up a home for yourself and your dependent(s) or other qualifying individuals. See line E below.

Nonwage income. If you have a large amount of nonwage income, such as interest or dividends, you should consider making estimated tax payments using Form 1040-ES. Otherwise, you may owe additional tax.

Two earners/two jobs. If you have a working spouse or more than one job, figure the total number of allowances you are entitled to claim on all jobs using worksheets from only one Form W-4. Your withholding will usually be most accurate when all allowances are claimed on the Form W-4 prepared for the highest paying job and zero allowances are claimed for the others.

Check your withholding. After your Form W-4 takes effect, use Pub. 919 to see how the dollar amount you are having withheld compares to your estimated total annual tax. Get Pub. 919 especially if you used the Two-Earner/Two-Job Worksheet and your earnings exceed $150,000 (Single) or $200,000 (Married).

Recent name change? If your name on line 1 differs from that shown on your social security card, call 1-800-772-1213 for a new social security card.

Personal Allowances Worksheet

A	Enter "1" for yourself if no one else can claim you as a dependent	**A** _____
B	Enter "1" if: ● You are single and have only one job; or ● You are married, have only one job, and your spouse does not work; or ● Your wages from a second job or your spouse's wages (or the total of both) are $1,000 or less.	**B** _____
C	Enter "1" for your spouse. But, you may choose to enter -0- if you are married and have either a working spouse or more than one job. (This may help you avoid having too little tax withheld.)	**C** _____
D	Enter number of dependents (other than your spouse or yourself) you will claim on your tax return	**D** _____
E	Enter "1" if you will file as head of household on your tax return (see conditions under Head of household above)	**E** _____
F	Enter "1" if you have at least $1,500 of child or dependent care expenses for which you plan to claim a credit	**F** _____
G	**Child Tax Credit:** ● If your total income will be between $20,000 and $50,000 ($23,000 and $63,000 if married), enter "1" for each eligible child. ● If your total income will be between $50,000 and $80,000 ($63,000 and $115,000 if married), enter "1" if you have two eligible children, enter "2" if you have three or four eligible children, or enter "3" if you have five or more eligible children . . .	**G** _____
H	Add lines A through G and enter total here. Note: This amount may be different from the number of exemptions you claim on your return. ▶ **H**	_____

For accuracy, complete all worksheets that apply.

● If you plan to itemize or claim adjustments to income and want to reduce your withholding, see the Deductions and Adjustments Worksheet on page 2.

● If you are **single**, have more than one job and your combined earnings from all jobs exceed $32,000, **OR** if you are **married** and have a working spouse or more than one job and the combined earnings from all jobs exceed $55,000, see the Two-Earner/Two-Job Worksheet on page 2 to avoid having too little tax withheld.

● If neither of the above situations applies, **stop here** and enter the number from line H on line 5 of Form W-4 below.

STF FED8105F.1

Cut here and give the certificate to your employer. Keep the top part for your records.

Form **W-4** Department of the Treasury Internal Revenue Service	**Employee's Withholding Allowance Certificate** ▶ For Privacy Act and Paperwork Reduction Act Notice, see page 2.	OMB No. 1545-0010 **1999**

1 Type or print your first name and middle initial	Last name	2 Your social security number

Home address (number and street or rural route)	3 ☐ Single ☐ Married ☐ Married, but withhold at higher Single rate. **Note:** *If married, but legally separated, or spouse is a nonresident alien, check the Single box.*
City or town, state, and ZIP code	4 If your last name differs from that on your social security card, check here. **You must call 1-800-772-1213 for a new card** . . . . ▶ ☐

5	Total number of allowances you are claiming (from line H above or from the worksheets on page 2 if they apply)	5	
6	Additional amount, if any, you want withheld from each paycheck	6	$

7 I claim exemption from withholding for 1999, and I certify that I meet **BOTH** of the following conditions for exemption:

● Last year I had a right to a refund of **ALL** Federal income tax withheld because I had **NO** tax liability **AND**

● This year I expect a refund of **ALL** Federal income tax withheld because I expect to have **NO** tax liability.

If you meet both conditions, enter "EXEMPT" here . . . . ▶ | 7 |

Under penalties of perjury, I certify that I am entitled to the number of withholding allowances claimed on this certificate, or I am entitled to claim exempt status.

Employee's signature (Form is not valid unless you sign it) ▶ _____ Date ▶ _____

8 Employer's name and address (Employer: Complete 8 and 10 only if sending to the IRS)	9 Office code (optional)	10 Employer identification number

ISA

Form W-4 (1999)   Page **2**

Deductions and Adjustments Worksheet

Note: *Use this worksheet only if you plan to itemize deductions or claim adjustments to income on your 1999 tax return.*

1   Enter an estimate of your 1999 itemized deductions. These include qualifying home mortgage interest, charitable contributions, state and local taxes (but not sales taxes), medical expenses in excess of 7.5% of your income, and miscellaneous deductions. (For 1999, you may have to reduce your itemized deductions if your income is over $126,600 ($63,300 if married filing separately). Get Pub. 919 for details.) . . . . **1** $ _____

2   Enter: { $7,200 if married filing jointly or qualifying widow(er)
             $6,350 if head of household   } . . . . **2** $ _____
             $4,300 if single
             $3,600 if married filing separately

3   Subtract line 2 from line 1. If line 2 is greater than line 1, enter -0- . . . . **3** $ _____

4   Enter an estimate of your 1999 adjustments to income, including alimony, deductible IRA contributions, and student loan interest . . . . **4** $ _____

5   Add lines 3 and 4 and enter the total . . . . **5** $ _____

6   Enter an estimate of your 1999 nonwage income (such as dividends or interest) . . . . **6** $ _____

7   Subtract line 6 from line 5. Enter the result, but not less than -0- . . . . **7** $ _____

8   Divide the amount on line 7 by $3,000 and enter the result here. Drop any fraction . . . . **8** _____

9   Enter the number from Personal Allowances Worksheet, line H, on page 1 . . . . **9** _____

10 Add lines 8 and 9 and enter the total here. If you plan to use the Two-Earner/Two-Job Worksheet, also enter this total on line 1 below. Otherwise, stop here and enter this total on Form W-4, line 5, on page 1 . . . . **10** _____

Two-Earner/Two-Job Worksheet

Note: *Use this worksheet only if the instructions for line H on page 1 direct you here.*

1   Enter the number from line H on page 1 (or from line 10 above if you used the Deductions and Adjustments Worksheet)   **1** _____

2   Find the number in Table 1 below that applies to the LOWEST paying job and enter it here . . . . **2** _____

3   If line 1 is GREATER THAN OR EQUAL TO line 2, subtract line 2 from line 1. Enter the result here (if zero, enter -0-) and on Form W-4, line 5, page 1. DO NOT use the rest of this worksheet . . . . **3** _____

Note: *If line 1 is LESS THAN line 2, enter -0- on Form W-4, line 5, on page 1. Complete lines 4 - 9 to calculate the additional withholding amount necessary to avoid a year end tax bill.*

4   Enter the number from line 2 of this worksheet . . . . **4** _____

5   Enter the number from line 1 of this worksheet . . . . **5** _____

6   Subtract line 5 from line 4 . . . . **6** _____

7   Find the amount in Table 2 below that applies to the HIGHEST paying job and enter it here . . . . **7** $ _____

8   Multiply line 7 by line 6 and enter the result here. This is the additional annual withholding amount needed . . . . **8** $ _____

9   Divide line 8 by the number of pay periods remaining in 1999. (For example, divide by 26 if you are paid every other week and you complete this form in December 1998.) Enter the result here and on Form W-4, line 6, page 1. This is the additional amount to be withheld from each paycheck . . . . **9** $ _____

Table 1: Two-Earner/Two-Job Worksheet

Married Filing Jointly				All Others			
If wages from **LOWEST** paying job are —	Enter on line 2 above	If wages from **LOWEST** paying job are —	Enter on line 2 above	If wages from **LOWEST** paying job are —	Enter on line 2 above	If wages from **LOWEST** paying job are —	Enter on line 2 above
$0 - $4,000	0	40,001 - 45,000	8	$0 - $5,000	0	65,001 - 80,000	8
4,001 - 7,000	1	45,001 - 54,000	9	5,001 - 11,000	1	80,001 - 100,000	9
7,001 - 12,000	2	54,001 - 62,000	10	11,001 - 16,000	2	100,001 and over	10
12,001 - 18,000	3	62,001 - 70,000	11	16,001 - 21,000	3		
18,001 - 24,000	4	70,001 - 85,000	12	21,001 - 25,000	4		
24,001 - 28,000	5	85,001 - 100,000	13	25,001 - 40,000	5		
28,001 - 35,000	6	100,001 - 110,000	14	40,001 - 50,000	6		
35,001 - 40,000	7	110,001 and over	15	50,001 - 65,000	7		

Table 2: Two-Earner/Two-Job Worksheet

Married Filing Jointly		All Others	
If wages from **HIGHEST** paying job are —	Enter on line 7 above	If wages from **HIGHEST** paying job are —	Enter on line 7 above
$0 - $50,000	$400	$0 - $30,000	$400
50,001 - 100,000	770	30,001 - 60,000	770
100,001 - 130,000	850	60,001 - 120,000	850
130,001 - 240,000	1,000	120,001 - 250,000	1,000
240,001 and over	1,100	250,001 and over	1,100

receive or expect a refund. The exercises are based upon the information in Publication 15, *Circular E, Employer's Tax Guide*. Using the percentage method of withholding, you can determine exactly what happens to a given paycheck upon claiming a specified number of allowances. The percentage method uses your income and the tax rates to determine the amount to withhold. This system can pinpoint the amount of withholding to cover your tax debt. The percentage method works for any number of withholding allowances and any amount of wages. This overcomes the handicap of the wage bracket method that is limited to a maximum of ten allowances.

Under the percentage method, each allowance claimed is assigned a value. The value increases as the number of pay periods in a year decrease. For example, in a weekly payroll period, each allowance is worth $52.88. In a monthly payroll period, each allowance is worth $229.17. The table below, taken from page 32 of the IRS' 1999 Publication 15, *Circular E*, shows the value of each allowance for 1999 withholding periods. You must check the current edition of *Circular E* for years after 1999.

Table of Allowance Values--1999 Percentage Method Withholding

Payroll Period	One Withholding Allowance
Weekly	$ 52.88
Biweekly	105.77
Semimonthly	114.58
Monthly	229.17
Quarterly	687.50
Semiannually	1,375.00
Annually	2,750.00
Daily or miscellaneous (each Day of the payroll period)	10.58

Use the following three steps to figure the income tax withholding using the percentage method:

a. Multiply the value of one withholding allowance for your payroll period by the number of allowances claimed on the W-4. Use the chart to determine the value for your payroll period. If you claim six withholding allowances and you are paid weekly, the product is $317.28 (six allowances multiplied by $52.88, the value of one allowance for a weekly payroll period).

b. Subtract the amount in paragraph (a) from your gross wages. If your gross wages are $650 per week, subtract $317.28 from the gross to arrive at the amount of wages subject to withholding, which is $332.72 ($650 gross wages minus $317.28, the allowance amount).

c. Using the wages subject to withholding, in this case, $332.72, refer to the appropriate table on the following two pages of this book. For example, a single person with a weekly payroll period refers to Table 1. A married person with a biweekly payroll period uses Table 2. Using Table 1 as an example, we determine from that table that the amount withheld from the weekly pay in this example is $42. This is ascertained by taking the amount subject to withholding ($332.72) and reading across the table to find the amount to be withheld. The table says to withhold 15 percent of the amount in excess of $51 but not over $525. Our amount is $332. The calculation appears as follows: $332.72 minus $51 equals $281.72 multiplied by 15 percent equals $42.25. Products should be rounded to the next highest or lowest whole number. In our example, withholding at this rate leads to $2,184 of withholding over the span of twelve months.

Using this simple formula and the tables provided, you can adjust your withholding allowances upward or downward to match your tax liability. Be sure to keep a record or worksheet of how you calculated your allowances. Under certain circumstances, the IRS or your employer may question your W-4. Make sure you can justify all the allowances claimed on the form. If you cannot, the IRS may instruct your employer to disregard the form and withhold as though you are a single person with no allowances. That means up to half your income

Tables for Percentage Method of Withholding
(For Wages Paid in 1999)

TABLE 1—WEEKLY Payroll Period

(a) SINGLE person (including head of household)—

If the amount of wages (after subtracting withholding allowances) is: / The amount of income tax to withhold is:

Not over $51 . . . . . $0

Over—	But not over—		of excess over—
$51	—$525	. 15%	—$51
$525	—$1,125	. $71.10 plus 28%	—$525
$1,125	—$2,535	. $239.10 plus 31%	—$1,125
$2,535	—$5,475	. $676.20 plus 36%	—$2,535
$5,475	. . . . .	. $1,734.60 plus 39.6%	—$5,475

(b) MARRIED person—

If the amount of wages (after subtracting withholding allowances) is: / The amount of income tax to withhold is:

Not over $124 . . . . . $0

Over—	But not over—		of excess over—
$124	—$913	. 15%	—$124
$913	—$1,894	. $118.35 plus 28%	—$913
$1,894	—$3,135	. $393.03 plus 31%	—$1,894
$3,135	—$5,531	. $777.74 plus 36%	—$3,135
$5,531	. . . . .	. $1,640.30 plus 39.6%	—$5,531

TABLE 2—BIWEEKLY Payroll Period

(a) SINGLE person (including head of household)—

If the amount of wages (after subtracting withholding allowances) is: / The amount of income tax to withhold is:

Not over $102 . . . . . $0

Over—	But not over—		of excess over—
$102	—$1,050	. 15%	—$102
$1,050	—$2,250	. $142.20 plus 28%	—$1,050
$2,250	—$5,069	. $478.20 plus 31%	—$2,250
$5,069	—$10,950	. $1,352.09 plus 36%	—$5,069
$10,950	. . . . .	. $3,469.25 plus 39.6%	—$10,950

(b) MARRIED person—

If the amount of wages (after subtracting withholding allowances) is: / The amount of income tax to withhold is:

Not over $248 . . . . . $0

Over—	But not over—		of excess over—
$248	—$1,827	. 15%	—$248
$1,827	—$3,788	. $236.85 plus 28%	—$1,827
$3,788	—$6,269	. $785.93 plus 31%	—$3,788
$6,269	—$11,062	. $1,555.04 plus 36%	—$6,269
$11,062	. . . . .	. $3,280.52 plus 39.6%	—$11,062

TABLE 3—SEMIMONTHLY Payroll Period

(a) SINGLE person (including head of household)—

If the amount of wages (after subtracting withholding allowances) is: / The amount of income tax to withhold is:

Not over $110 . . . . . $0

Over—	But not over—		of excess over—
$110	—$1,138	. 15%	—$110
$1,138	—$2,438	. $154.20 plus 28%	—$1,138
$2,438	—$5,492	. $518.20 plus 31%	—$2,438
$5,492	—$11,863	. $1,464.94 plus 36%	—$5,492
$11,863	. . . . .	. $3,758.50 plus 39.6%	—$11,863

(b) MARRIED person—

If the amount of wages (after subtracting withholding allowances) is: / The amount of income tax to withhold is:

Not over $269 . . . . . $0

Over—	But not over—		of excess over—
$269	—$1,979	. 15%	—$269
$1,979	—$4,104	. $256.50 plus 28%	—$1,979
$4,104	—$6,792	. $851.50 plus 31%	—$4,104
$6,792	—$11,983	. $1,684.78 plus 36%	—$6,792
$11,983	. . . . .	. $3,553.54 plus 39.6%	—$11,983

TABLE 4—MONTHLY Payroll Period

(a) SINGLE person (including head of household)—

If the amount of wages (after subtracting withholding allowances) is: / The amount of income tax to withhold is:

Not over $221 . . . . . $0

Over—	But not over—		of excess over—
$221	—$2,275	. 15%	—$221
$2,275	—$4,875	. $308.10 plus 28%	—$2,275
$4,875	—$10,983	. $1,036.10 plus 31%	—$4,875
$10,983	—$23,725	. $2,929.58 plus 36%	—$10,983
$23,725	. . . . .	. $7,516.70 plus 39.6%	—$23,725

(b) MARRIED person—

If the amount of wages (after subtracting withholding allowances) is: / The amount of income tax to withhold is:

Not over $538 . . . . . $0

Over—	But not over—		of excess over—
$538	—$3,958	. 15%	—$538
$3,958	—$8,208	. $513.00 plus 28%	—$3,958
$8,208	—$13,583	. $1,703.00 plus 31%	—$8,208
$13,583	—$23,967	. $3,369.25 plus 36%	—$13,583
$23,967	. . . . .	. $7,107.49 plus 39.6%	—$23,967

Tables for Percentage Method of Withholding (Continued)
(For Wages Paid in 1999)

TABLE 5—QUARTERLY Payroll Period

(a) SINGLE person (including head of household)—

If the amount of wages (after subtracting withholding allowances) is: / The amount of income tax to withhold is:

Not over $663 . . . . $0

Over—	But not over—		of excess over—
$663	—$6,825	15%	—$663
$6,825	—$14,625	$924.30 plus 28%	—$6,825
$14,625	—$32,950	$3,108.30 plus 31%	—$14,625
$32,950	—$71,175	$8,789.05 plus 36%	—$32,950
$71,175	. . . . .	$22,550.05 plus 39.6%	—$71,175

(b) MARRIED person—

If the amount of wages (after subtracting withholding allowances) is: / The amount of income tax to withhold is:

Not over $1,613 . . . . $0

Over—	But not over—		of excess over—
$1,613	—$11,875	15%	—$1,613
$11,875	—$24,625	$1,539.30 plus 28%	—$11,875
$24,625	—$40,750	$5,109.30 plus 31%	—$24,625
$40,750	—$71,900	$10,108.05 plus 36%	—$40,750
$71,900	. . . . .	$21,322.05 plus 39.6%	—$71,900

TABLE 6—SEMIANNUAL Payroll Period

(a) SINGLE person (including head of household)—

If the amount of wages (after subtracting withholding allowances) is: / The amount of income tax to withhold is:

Not over $1,325 . . . . $0

Over—	But not over—		of excess over—
$1,325	—$13,650	15%	—$1,325
$13,650	—$29,250	$1,848.75 plus 28%	—$13,650
$29,250	—$65,900	$6,216.75 plus 31%	—$29,250
$65,900	—$142,350	$17,578.25 plus 36%	—$65,900
$142,350	. . . . .	$45,100.25 plus 39.6%	—$142,350

(b) MARRIED person—

If the amount of wages (after subtracting withholding allowances) is: / The amount of income tax to withhold is:

Not over $3,225 . . . . $0

Over—	But not over—		of excess over—
$3,225	—$23,750	15%	—$3,225
$23,750	—$49,250	$3,078.75 plus 28%	—$23,750
$49,250	—$81,500	$10,218.75 plus 31%	—$49,250
$81,500	—$143,800	$20,216.25 plus 36%	—$81,500
$143,800	. . . . .	$42,644.25 plus 39.6%	—$143,800

TABLE 7—ANNUAL Payroll Period

(a) SINGLE person (including head of household)—

If the amount of wages (after subtracting withholding allowances) is: / The amount of income tax to withhold is:

Not over $2,650 . . . . $0

Over—	But not over—		of excess over—
$2,650	—$27,300	15%	—$2,650
$27,300	—$58,500	$3,697.50 plus 28%	—$27,300
$58,500	—$131,800	$12,433.50 plus 31%	—$58,500
$131,800	—$284,700	$35,156.50 plus 36%	—$131,800
$284,700	. . . . .	$90,200.50 plus 39.6%	—$284,700

(b) MARRIED person—

If the amount of wages (after subtracting withholding allowances) is: / The amount of income tax to withhold is:

Not over $6,450 . . . . $0

Over—	But not over—		of excess over—
$6,450	—$47,500	15%	—$6,450
$47,500	—$98,500	$6,157.50 plus 28%	—$47,500
$98,500	—$163,000	$20,437.50 plus 31%	—$98,500
$163,000	—$287,600	$40,432.50 plus 36%	—$163,000
$287,600	. . . . .	$85,288.50 plus 39.6%	—$287,600

TABLE 8—DAILY or MISCELLANEOUS Payroll Period

(a) SINGLE person (including head of household)—

If the amount of wages (after subtracting withholding allowances) divided by the number of days in the payroll period is: / The amount of income tax to withhold per day is:

Not over $10.20 . . . . $0

Over—	But not over—		of excess over—
$10.20	—$105.00	15%	—$10.20
$105.00	—$225.00	$14.22 plus 28%	—$105.00
$225.00	—$506.90	$47.82 plus 31%	—$225.00
$506.90	—$1,095.00	$135.21 plus 36%	—$506.90
$1,095.00	. . . . .	$346.93 plus 39.6%	—$1,095.00

(b) MARRIED person—

If the amount of wages (after subtracting withholding allowances) divided by the number of days in the payroll period is: / The amount of income tax to withhold per day is:

Not over $24.80 . . . . $0

Over—	But not over—		of excess over—
$24.80	—$182.70	15%	—$24.80
$182.70	—$378.80	$23.69 plus 28%	—$182.70
$378.80	—$626.90	$78.60 plus 31%	—$378.80
$626.90	—$1,106.20	$155.51 plus 36%	—$626.90
$1,106.20	. . . . .	$328.06 plus 39.6%	—$1,106.20

could be lost to withholding. We discuss this issue more thoroughly in chapter 4, *Defending the W-4.*

If both you and your spouse work, you cannot double up on allowances. They can be claimed by either spouse or divided between the two. However, the sum of allowances on both W-4 Forms cannot exceed the total number allowed. If you are entitled to claim twelve, either spouse can claim twelve or each can claim six (or any other combination, the sum of which is twelve). But the total claimed cannot exceed twelve.

If you are self-employed, you must use caution and restraint with your budget because you are not subject to wage withholding. You are paid in full by customers or clients and bear the burden of paying your own taxes. You must make quarterly estimated payments of your current taxes. The payments are due April 15, June 15, September 15 and January 15 of the following year. Make the payments on IRS Form 1040 ES, *Individual Estimated Tax Payment Voucher*, a simple payment coupon. An example of Form 1040 ES is shown below.

Form **1040-ES** Department of the Treasury Internal Revenue Service	**1999** Payment Voucher **1**	OMB No. 1545-0087

File only if you are making a payment of estimated tax. Return this voucher with check or money order payable to the "**United States Treasury.**" Please write your social security number and "1999 Form 1040-ES" on your check or money order. Do not send cash. Enclose, but do not staple or attach, your payment with this voucher.

Calendar year — Due April 15, 1999

Amount of payment	Please type or print	Your first name and initial	Your last name	Your social security number
		If joint payment, complete for spouse		
		Spouse's first name and initial	Spouse's last name	Spouse's social security number
		Address (number, street, and apt. no.)		
$		City, state, and ZIP code (If a foreign address, enter city, province or state, postal code, and country.)		

For Privacy Act and Paperwork Reduction Act Notice, see instructions on page 5.

ISA

The best way for self-employed persons to cover estimated tax obligations is to ascertain their "effective tax rate" and make estimated payments based on that rate. The effective tax rate is the percentage of income you pay in total tax measured against your gross income, *before deductions*. This is how to compute your effective rate:

Start by determining your total federal tax for the preceding year, say 1998. Your total 1998 federal tax liability *includes* social security (otherwise known as self-employment taxes) and is the tax liability *before* applying payment credits. Suppose that number is $10,500 for purposes of illustration. Divide that number into your gross receipts for 1998, *before* considering any deductions or expenses whatsoever. Suppose your gross receipts were $60,000. By dividing $10,500 into $60,000, you arrive at a fraction, which is .175. Thus, .175, or 17.5 percent, is your effective federal tax rate. It means that 17.5 percent of *every dollar* you earn goes to federal taxes. Because of the graduated income tax rates, some of the money is taxed at 15 percent and some is taxed at 28 percent. The more deductions you have, the less will be your effective tax rate.

After finding your effective federal tax rate, do the same for state income taxes. Suppose your state effective tax rate is 7 percent. You must now set aside a total of 24.5 percent (17.5 federal plus 7 percent state) *of every dollar you earn* to cover your income tax burden. If you earn $60,000 gross, your monthly income is about $5,000. At 24.5 percent, you must set aside $1,225 ($5,000 x .245) per month to cover your *current* federal and state income and social security tax debt. On a quarterly basis, send a payment to the IRS equal to three monthly estimates, or $3,675 ($1,225 x 3), using Form 1040 ES, the payment coupon. Make a similar payment to the state using the coupon provided by your state revenue department. State estimated payments are also made quarterly.

I recommend self-employed persons establish a separate bank account to handle estimated taxes. That way, the money is not commingled with business or personal operating funds and you are less likely to spend it. In addition, you get into the habit of writing a monthly check for taxes. That way, they become a real part of your budget and you therefore do not find yourself behind the eight ball on April 15.

Monitor Your Circumstances

Form W-4 is a living document. Regularly review your tax situation and change your W-4 accordingly. Too many people sign the W-4 when they are hired, then never look at it again. This is a mistake. Consider the W-4 a tool to balance your withholding to match your tax liability.

Major changes in your personal life should immediately occasion a review of your W-4. If, for example, you get married or divorced; you have a new baby or a child moves out on his own; you start a new business; you purchase a new home or pay off an existing mortgage; your state income or real estate taxes are adjusted substantially one way or the other; you incur substantial medical expenses, or; you suffer a casualty loss or an investment fails. These are just of few of the things that impact your tax liability and should be considered for withholding purposes.

Likewise, self-employed persons must review their circumstances on a quarterly basis, at about the time the next 1040 ES is due for filing. The largest factor to consider is quarterly income. Many self-employed people earn income seasonally or in some other imprecise manner. If income substantially rises or falls during a given quarter, take that into consideration. In addition, consider the purchase or sale of equipment or facilities; the hiring or laying off of employees; the sale of inventory items; operational expenses such as utilities, postage, rent, printing, etc. Keep tabs on these items as you move through the year so you do not get caught short or over-pay. Later, I discuss a number of strategies the self-employed can use effectively to pay less taxes.

What to do in December

At the very least, your financial circumstances should always be reviewed in December. This is when to begin the tax return preparation process. Do not wait until April or even February, after you have your W-2 Forms in hand. By using the recordkeeping techniques we discuss in the final two chapters of this book, you should be able to rough out your return before the end of the year. That way, you can see exactly where you stand with the IRS before the new year begins. This gives you the ability to adjust your W-4 on January 2 if necessary. That way, you begin the new year with your money in your pocket--where it belongs.

CHAPTER THREE
How to Get Your Refund Now

Where would you rather have your money, in your own possession or in the IRS' possession? The answer is clear and easy but few understand the procedures available to accomplish it. In this chapter, I show you exactly how to use the withholding process to begin getting your refund now, even if you already received one this year. When you have possession of your own money, you are free to use and enjoy that money in ways that enhance your savings or standard of living. In the later chapters of this book, I explain ways you can double or triple the real value of your refund by putting it to work for you.

How to Claim Exemption From Withholding

First, let us examine the circumstances under which a person may actually be entirely exempt from withholding. In such cases, the withholding process stops and one receives his paycheck largely intact. The exemption I speak of is offered under code section 3402(n) but applies only to federal income taxes. Even under the exemption expressed in the statute, withholding continues for social security and state income taxes where applicable.

Every year, millions of people otherwise not required to pay income taxes file tax returns to "get a refund." By that I mean they do not earn enough money to be required to pay income taxes yet they must file just to get a refund of taxes withheld. Those who fall into this situation are always low-income wage earners. They may be students, single mothers with part-time jobs or retired persons supplementing social security benefits. In all cases, they earn little income but lose a portion to wage withholding which they cannot get back for well over a year.

To add insult to injury, not only do they lose the use of their money for over a year but they must incur the time, hassle and expense of preparing and filing a tax return just to prove they owe no taxes. Ironically, in many cases, these people did not even earn enough money to be legally required to file a tax return. They file solely to get their money back. This is one of the great inefficiencies of the system. Why subject yourself to wage deductions for taxes you do not owe solely to create the need to file a return you are not required to file? It seems to be a lot of wasted time, effort and resources.

One way to avoid the circuitous parade of paperwork is (for those who qualify) to claim exemption from withholding. Code section 3402(n) provides for the exemption when (1) you incurred no liability for income taxes the preceding taxable year, and (2) you reasonably anticipate incurring no liability for income taxes in the current taxable year. Please note that to be exempt from withholding, you must meet *both* criteria. Let me illustrate how they apply.

Suppose you are a full-time student with a part-time job. Suppose 1999 is the "current taxable year." During the course of 1998 (the "preceding taxable year"), you owed the IRS nothing due to low earnings. You received a refund of all withholding. That is not to say you received a partial refund of withholding taxes. Rather, you received a full refund of all your withholding and ended up at net zero in terms of federal income taxes. As such, you incurred no liability for taxes for 1998, the preceding taxable year.

In 1999, the current year, you expect to earn about $5,000. As a single person, you are not required to file a 1999 income tax return unless you earn more than $6,950. Therefore, you would clearly owe no federal income taxes on $5,000 of income. As a result, you can "reasonably anticipate" that you will have "no liability for income taxes in the current taxable year."

Under these circumstances, you meet the two criteria of code section 3402(n) and are permitted to declare legally that you are exempt from withholding. The exemption declaration is made on Form W-4. To make the declaration, complete lines 1-3 and line 7, then sign the W-4. Upon submission to your employer, federal income tax withholding stops.

By using this strategy, you get your refund during the course of the year, when you need it and at a time when you can best put it to work. What is more, you do not incur the costs in terms of time, hassle and money of preparing and filing a return, then waiting for the refund.

Get Two Refunds this Year

Even those who do not meet the two-pronged test to be exempt from withholding can achieve what amounts to the same thing through another means. I speak of increasing withholding allowances sufficiently to stop withholding in its entirety. This procedure allows you to get another refund now even though you may already have received one this year. Essentially, you get two refunds in one year. This is how it works.

Suppose your 1998 income tax liability was $5,000 and you paid $6,000 in withholding. In April or May of 1999, you received a $1,000 refund. Based on this example, you pay estimated taxes through wage withholding at the rate of $500 per month. By the end of October, 1999, ten months into the year, you would have paid $5,000 in withholding, an amount equal to your total 1998 tax debt. With two months of the year still remaining, your 1999 tax debt is paid in full, assuming your financial circumstances have not dramatically changed. You are on track for another $1,000 refund.

But why not get your refund now instead of waiting until April or May of the following year? Why not have it available now to use or invest? The problem is you cannot claim the exemption from withholding I just described above for two reasons. First, you incurred a tax liability last year, a total of $5,000. Remember, even though you received a $1,000 refund, you paid a total of $6,000 in withholding. Secondly, you reasonably anticipate a tax liability in the current year. Because your circumstances have not changed, you will owe about $5,000 for the current year.

So, while you cannot claim the exemption described earlier, you can increase the number of allowances on your W-4 Form to stop withholding entirely. The process is very simple. Just refer to IRS Publication 15, *Circular E, Employer's Tax Guide* and chapter two of this book, under the heading, *Fine Tuning Your Withholding.* Use the procedures described there to find the number of allowances needed to stop withholding. That number is probably two or three more allowances than what you currently claim. Adjust your W-4 to claim the number required to stop withholding and submit it to your employer. In the next two months, you will take home an additional $1,000 of net income. You get your tax refund now instead of waiting. But take note: you must remember to change your W-4 in January of the following year to accommodate the correct withholding scenario applicable at that time. *Do not* continue with zero withholding. See the heading below entitled, *What to do in December.*

By following the process just described, you not only get your refund now but you make your life easier and save yourself money as well. All across the nation, millions of people file their tax returns electronically. The IRS sells the idea of electronic filing by promising a speedy refund. But tax professionals often charge a fee for electronic filing. As such, you pay for the privilege of getting back your own money from the IRS. Would you pay me $50 just to get back the $1,000 I owe you and must pay anyway? Why pay such a fee to anybody else?

But the additional costs do not stop there. We regularly see citizens obtaining "tax refund" loans from lenders in the spring of the year. You see the advertisements everywhere. You can bring your tax return to certain financial institutions that lend money based upon the amount of your refund. In exchange for the cash now, you agree to re-pay the principal with interest when you receive the refund. Would you pay me interest on a $1,000 loan that does nothing but allow you to use your own money? Why pay it to a bank?

Smart tax professionals and savvy bankers have found very creative ways to get into your pocket. However, you have total control over your refund. You do not have to pay a banker or tax preparer for the privilege of using your own money. Just use the steps outlined here and you can get your refund anytime you want--free of charge.

Get a Refund When You Do Not Owe Taxes

Some time ago, Congress enacted a legal provision designed to help the "working poor." These are people with families who, though they have jobs, make little income each year and often struggle to make ends meet. The Earned Income Credit is designed to operate as a refundable credit intended to lower the tax bite of the working poor. As a refundable credit, the earned income credit can have the effect of reducing your tax liability below zero. That is to say, not only can it wipe out what you owe in taxes entirely but it can also give you a refund even when you did not owe any tax at all.

When you qualify for the earned income credit, you claim it on your tax return at the end of the year. It can increase the size of your refund. But you do not have to wait until April to claim it. If you qualify for the earned income credit, you can receive advance payment of the credit from your employer through the wage withholding system. In this way, the withholding system actually works in reverse. Instead of taking money from your paycheck, you actually receive extra money.

The rules for determining who qualifies for the earned income credit are set forth in IRS Publication 596, *Earned Income Credit*. Generally, you must be married with children or the head of a household. There are strict income limits that are modified from year to year. The current edition of Publication 596 sets forth all the rules. To claim the refund credit in each paycheck, submit a correctly completed Form W-4 to your employer. On the basis of the information in the W-5, *Earned Income Credit Advance Payment Certificate* (a separate form specifically for claiming advance payment of the credit), your employer makes advance payments to you of the earned income credit in each paycheck.

What to Do in December

Anytime you substantially adjust your W-4 or claim exemption from withholding, you must review your circumstances periodically. If, for example, you claim exemption from withholding, carefully review your circumstances in December. Determine whether, in the following year, you can reasonably anticipate continuing to meet the two requirements needed to justify the exempt claim. If your circumstances change and say, you will be working full-time the following year, be prepared to change the W-4 to reflect those circumstances. Form W-5 must be revised at the end of each year. You cannot move into a new tax year with a W-5 covering the previous year.

Periodic reviews are more important if you used the allowance method to stop withholding. One can quickly and easily become accustomed to an extra $500 per month in take-home pay. And this is fine, as long as the money is *after-tax* income. However, if you do not pay close attention to your situation, you can end up receiving *before-tax* dollars in your pay. That means for every $1,000 in before-tax money you receive, you owe the IRS $280 (if you are in the 28 percent bracket). It is easy to see how this can become a real problem if the pattern continues for any length of time.

Because you have the right to adjust your W-4 on a regular basis, you have the obligation to monitor your situation to keep matters under control. Do not make the mistake of diverting money that should be earmarked for taxes to some other use. I can think of no situation that justifies placing tax money at risk or using it in some fashion that might jeopardize your ability to pay the correct amount in full and on time.

On the other hand, the rewards are great for those who pay attention to these teachings.

CHAPTER FOUR
Audit-Proofing and Penalty-Proofing Your Form W-4

The IRS is very defensive of its withholding tax system. The withholding system is referred to by tax planners as a "safety net." It means that without the system in place, many people might not pay their taxes. In fact, that is exactly why withholding was created in the first place. The theory was that people would be willing to foot almost any expense if they could pay it in installments. However, if they were asked to pay in a lump sum, there would be wailing and gnashing of teeth and, no doubt, much tax evasion. It is undeniable that our tax burden could never have climbed as high as it is now without the tool of wage withholding.

As a result, the IRS is very protective of the system. The agency goes to great lengths to ensure that citizens undergo the correct amount of withholding and it does so in two primary ways. First, it reviews "questionable" W-4 Forms. A questionable W-4 is one which, on its face, does not appear to be accurate. Secondly, it imposes penalties upon those who file false W-4s or otherwise fail to withhold properly. These facts often induce people to fail to take advantage of their rights. However, when you understand the rules, you eliminate the risk.

In the final chapter of this book, I explain a system that has been very successful in audit-proofing and penalty-proofing income tax returns. The sum and substance of the strategy is to provide information with the return that answers any potential questions raised in the return. That way, the IRS has all the information it needs to pass upon the correctness of a tax return without the need of a face-to-face audit. Moreover, even if it should transpire that you made an honest mistake on your tax return, by disclosing your position to the IRS in the return itself, you evidence good faith and a lack of intent to cheat. That in turn acts as a bar to any penalty the IRS may wish to assert as a result of the error.

Why not use the same procedures to audit-proof and penalty-proof your W-4? In this way, you claim the withholding status you are legally entitled to claim, you reduce your withholding to its lowest legal level and you do it without risk that the IRS will either attempt to alter your W-4 or penalize you for submitting it. While there is much more discussion in chapter ten on audit-proofing your tax return, let us discuss here the process of audit-proofing a W-4 Form.

How W-4 Forms are Reviewed

Under IRS regulations, an employer is not required to be a W-4 cop. That is, it is not your employer's responsibility to review your financial circumstances to ensure that your W-4 claim is accurate. Under normal circumstances, the employer accepts the W-4 as filed and withholds on the basis of the allowances claimed. However, in narrow circumstances, a Form W-4 might appear to the employer to be "questionable." In that case, the employer might inquire of you why such a form was submitted or might send the form to the IRS for a determination of its accuracy.

An employer sends a W-4 to the IRS for review only if the employer has serious questions about the form's legitimacy. Specifically, the IRS asks employers to take notice of W-4 forms on which one claims more than ten withholding allowances or claims to be exempt from withholding but the employee earns more than $200 per week. This is not to say that such claims are wrong. Provided the employee can explain how he arrived at the claim and can show that it is legitimate, the W-4 is proper and will be allowed to stand.

Audit-Proofing the W-4

Now that we know certain W-4 Forms may be examined more closely by your employer and perhaps the IRS, the question is how do you avoid an "audit" of the W-4? The answer is quite simple. Earlier I stated that the forms which are reviewed by the employer and potentially sent to the IRS are those which appear to be "questionable." That is, those forms which on their face, may not be correct. The key, therefore, to avoiding the W-4 audit is to provide information with the W-4 form that proves it is correct.

In other words, document your claims of allowances or exempt status with attachments to the W-4 itself. In this way, you provide information with the W-4 that answers any potential questions raised by it. By doing so, your W-4 is not "questionable." Rather, the claims are documented and your employer or potentially the IRS can plainly see that, given the facts of your case, you are entitled to the claim made on the form.

Documenting the Form W-4

Documenting the accuracy of your W-4 is very simple. Provided the claims in your W-4 are proper, you will have no problem. Keep in mind that our focus in chapters two and three was to eliminate over-withholding. You have no legal obligation to subject yourself to over-withholding. Provided you meet the level of estimated payments required by code section 6654 (see chapter two for the 90%/100% rule), your W-4 is proper and must be allowed to stand.

To document your W-4, attach worksheets directly to the form that shows the following:

a. the number of dependent exemptions you are entitled to claim on your current income tax return; and

b. All the calculations that went into determining the number of withholding allowances claimed in excess of dependent exemptions.

For example, suppose you claimed eleven allowances on your W-4 and five of them are attributable to dependent exemptions for yourself, your spouse and three children. That leaves six allowances that must be attributable to estimated itemized deductions, tax credits or other tax return items that lower your tax. Since each allowance has a value of $3,000, you must show that you have $18,000 (six allowances multiplied by $3,000) worth of claims in the current year that reduce your taxable income. These include mortgage interest payments, real estate taxes, child tax credits, etc. Please see the list of items in chapter two, under the heading, *Figuring Estimated Payments.*

If you claimed exemption from withholding by completing line 7 of the W-4, you must prove, a) you incurred no tax liability for the preceding year and, b) you anticipate incurring no tax for the current year. If you make such a claim, back it up with IRS Form 6450, *Questionnaire to Determine Exemption from Withholding.* An examination copy of this form is reproduced on the following two pages.

Form 6450 can help you but this is not a form the IRS talks about. Complete the form and attach it directly to your W-4 at the time of filing. Provide such additional information as is necessary to support your claim. If you filed a Form 1040 for the prior year, the return should show that you incurred no tax. Provide a copy as an attachment to Form 6450. If you did not file a return, provide a statement showing your total gross income and declaring that you were not required to file as a result of earning less than the legal filing requirement. If you have a W-2 form showing your total income for the prior year, attach that to Form 6450.

To prove you anticipate incurring no tax liability in the current year, provide a statement showing your current earnings and describe your factual circumstances. This statement should explain why, under the circumstances, you will not earn enough to incur a tax liability by the end of the year. It could be that you are a student working part-time, you have a seasonal job, you were injured and can work only a very few hours per week, etc. Anytime you can document a claim, such as an injury, do so to the fullest extent possible. Attach the statement to Form 6450.

If you used the allowance method to stop all withholding because you paid enough to cover your anticipated tax liability, you must prove that wage withholding to date has accounted for payment of your anticipated tax debt. You must show that your withholding covers the 90%/100% rule discussed in chapter two. The explanation should include a statement that you are fully aware of your obligation to undergo wage withholding in the proper amount and that you monitor your withholding on a regular basis, changing your W-4 as necessary based upon the

Form **6450** (Rev. March 1992)	Department of the Treasury – Internal Revenue Service **Questionnaire To Determine Exemption From Withholding**	Date

Your name	Your Social Security Number (as shown on the letter)
	If your name or social security number (SSN) is incorrect on the letter, or an asterisk (*) appears after the SSN, show your correct SSN and any former names in the boxes below.
	Your correct social security number
Phone number and best time to call	Former name(s) (Please print)

INSTRUCTIONS:

If you are claiming exempt status, please complete Part I of this form.

If you can be claimed as a dependent on another person's income tax return, complete Part II;

If you are claiming exemption from withholding based on a vow of poverty, complete Part III;

If you had income earned abroad, complete Part IV.

ALL must complete the enclosed Form W-4 including the appropriate worksheet(s) and return both forms in the enclosed envelope.

(DO NOT DETACH CERTIFICATE)

Part I – Qualifications for Claiming Exemption from Withholding

1. Last year, I had a right to a refund of ALL income tax withheld because I did not have any Federal income tax liability . . . . ☐ Yes ☐ No

2. This year, I expect to have a right to a refund of ALL income tax withheld because I do not expect to have any Federal income tax liability . . . . ☐ Yes ☐ No

3. Are you a resident alien? . . . . ☐ Yes ☐ No

4. If yes, give Visa Type _____ Date arrived in U.S. _____ Country _____

   (Visa types F, J, or M may not claim exempt status if compensation is received for personal services performed in the U.S.)

Part II – For Individuals Who Can Be Claimed on Another Person's Tax Return

5. Could you be claimed as dependent on another person's
   tax return last year? . . . . ☐ Yes ☐ No
   This year? . . . . ☐ Yes ☐ No

6. What was the total amount of your earned income last year?
   (Earned income is income from wages, salaries, professional fees, tips, and
   other compensation received for personal services you performed. It also
   includes any amount received as a scholarship that you must include in your
   income.) . . . . $ _____

7. What do you estimate your total earned income will be this year? . . . . $ _____

8. What was the total amount of your unearned income last year?
   (Unearned income is all income other than salaries, wages, tips, and personal
   service income. It includes interest, dividends, alimony, capital gains and losses,
   pensions) . . . . $ _____

9. What do you estimate your total unearned income will be this year? . . . . $ _____

Form **6450** (Rev. 3-92)

Part III – Claiming Exemption from Withholding Based on a Vow of Poverty

10. Are you a minister of a church? .... ☐ Yes ☐ No

11. Are you a member of a religious order? .... ☐ Yes ☐ No

12. Enter the name and address of the church or order.

    Name _____

    Street Address _____

    City, State, Zip _____

13. Did you have any salary or wages last year from outside
    the church or order? .... ☐ Yes ☐ No

    If yes, show the names of your outside employers and how much you expect
    to earn this year from employment outside the church or order.

Employer Name	Estimated Earnings This Year

Part IV – Foreign Issues

14. Are you eligible for the foreign earned income exclusion this year? .... ☐ Yes ☐ No

15. If yes, enter amount here (not to exceed $70,000) .... $ _____

    Also enter any housing exclusion deduction you are entitled to .... $ _____

Certification

Under penalties of perjury, I declare that I have examined this questionnaire
and, to the best of my knowledge and belief, it is true, correct, and complete.

Your signature	Date

circumstances. State that you have in the past and will continue to meet the 90%/100% rule as expressed in code section 6654. Also state that you file your returns on time every year.

Provided you can show that you are entitled to the status claimed on the W-4, there should be no question about the legitimacy of your claim. The employer will accept the form and that is the end of it.

In unusual cases, the employer may send your W-4 to the IRS for review. In that case, the agency reviews the form to determine if it is correct. Provided you have submitted all the documentation mentioned above, the IRS will have no problem accepting the W-4. This is the beauty of providing the information as attachments directly to the W-4. This way, the agency has everything at its fingertips needed to pass upon the merits of your claim without hassling you for additional information. In the event it does send a letter seeking explanations, provide complete and accurate explanations in a timely manner showing that your claims are legal and proper. That ends the inquiry.

Handling W-4 and Withholding Penalties

If you audit-proof and penalty-proof the W-4 as outlined above, you should never have to deal with W-4 or withholding penalties. However, one of the IRS' most consistent errors is the assessment of improper penalties. Therefore, you should understand the penalties that are available to the IRS and how to deal with a potentially improper assessment. Because people do not understand how the penalty process operates, most people faced with a penalty end up paying it even though it is probably improper.

Of the over 140 different penalty provisions of the tax code, there are two you must be aware of and understand in the context of our discussion thus far. The first one is the penalty for filing a false Form W-4 and the second is the penalty for underpaying estimated taxes. Let us address each of the two penalties in turn.

The False Withholding Certificate

Code section 6682(a) provides for a penalty of $500 for a Form W-4 that, 1) "results in a decrease" in the amount of tax withheld from your paycheck, and 2) for which "there was no reasonable basis" for the claim at the time it was made. Please note that the penalty does not apply to a mere "decrease" of withholding. The penalty applies only when there is a decrease *and* there is no reasonable basis for the claim. If you properly document the reasons why your withholding was decreased, you cannot properly be charged with this penalty.

There are three different approaches to handling this potential problem, depending upon the facts of your case. The first addresses a correct Form W-4 that is questioned by the IRS. The second deals with avoiding the penalty even if your Form W-4 is incorrect. The third applies when little or no tax is owed. I address each one in turn.

The Correct W-4. As I already stated, the penalty under code section 6682(a) applies only if there is "no reasonable basis" for the claim made in the W-4. In other words, when your claims of a particular number of allowances or exemption from withholding are supported by the facts of your case, the penalty cannot legitimately be assessed. If you followed the procedures set forth in chapters two and three, you not only have a "reasonable basis" for your claim, but you are able to document exactly how you arrived at that claim. As such, you cannot be penalized under code section 6682.

In response to the IRS' notice regarding the penalty under code section 6682, submit a letter in writing that explains:

a. How you determined your withholding status;

b. Specific facts and circumstances that justify your claim;

c. That your claim was made in good faith and based upon the reasonable cause as shown by the facts; and, most importantly,

d. That to your best knowledge as shown by the facts, you believe there is a "reasonable basis" for the claim. Emphasize that you did not file the form to unlawfully reduce your withholding nor did you do so believing you had no reasonable basis for the claim.

Promptly mail the letter via certified mail, return receipt requested, to the IRS at the address shown on its notice. Be careful to identify the letter as one in response to the Form W-4 inquiry and state that your letter is written to avoid or cancel the penalty under code section 6682.

The Incorrect W-4. It if turns out that your W-4 is in fact incorrect, you must take care to explain your actions. That way, you avoid the $500 penalty. The statute provides a two-pronged test for determining whether the penalty applies. The first is that the W-4 led to a reduction in withholding and the second is that "at the time the statement was made," there was no "reasonable basis" for making it. If your withholding statement is incorrect, you may nevertheless avoid the $500 penalty by setting forth, in writing, the specific facts and circumstances leading you to the conclusion that you had a "reasonable basis" for your claim.

All financial circumstances affecting your determination must be set forth in the letter. Please note: the law provides that the facts considered in determining whether there is a "reasonable basis" for the statement are the facts that existed at the time the statement was made. This is important because if the IRS examines your Form W-4, it does so several months--perhaps years--after you filed it. Thus, the IRS may apply current facts to the form in determining its validity. However, the statute is clear that the facts that apply in answering the "reasonable basis" question are those that existed "at the time" the statement was made. Take care to recite the facts existing at the time the form was filed in order to establish a "reasonable basis" for your claim. Be sure to keep all of your notes and worksheets used to establish the claim in the first place. These notes are critical to proving your "reasonable basis." By making this case, you avoid the $500 penalty.

When Little or no Tax is Owed. The third exception to the penalty is expressed in section 6682(b). That section provides that the penalty can be avoided if the taxes for the year in question are either equal to or less than the sum of, 1) all credits against the tax, such as child credits, etc., and 2) the withholding payments made against the taxes. In other words, if your total tax debt for the year is equal to or less than the combined total of your tax credits and withholding payments up to the time of filing the incorrect W-4, the penalty does not apply.

Underpayment of Estimated Taxes

As we examined in chapter two, code section 6654 establishes the amount of estimated taxes that must be paid during the year and provides a penalty for failure to make those payments. The statute also creates a number of defenses and a broad exception to the penalty that can apply in a great many cases. We examine the defenses and the exception in the remainder of this chapter.

Section 6654(d)(1) establishes the 90%/100% rule we examined earlier in this book. To review, one must make estimated payments equal to the lesser of 90 percent of the current year's taxes or 100 percent of the prior year's tax, whichever is less. Experience teaches that the IRS often assesses penalties in cases where they are simply not justified. By knowing how to challenge a potential penalty, you can avoid unjustified assessments. Let us examine the defenses to the penalty under code section 6654.

90%/100% Rule is Met. A man I knew worked for a large corporation in 1987. He earned an average income and paid approximately $4,000 in federal taxes. In 1988, he struck out on his own and scored with his business. His income rose substantially and his tax liability followed. In 1988, he owed income taxes in excess of $14,000. During the year, the self-employed man used Form 1040 ES to make estimated payments of his 1988 tax liability. He paid around $5,700 in four quarterly installments. At the time of filing his 1988 return, he paid the $8,300 balance in full.

Shortly thereafter, he received a notice from the IRS claiming he owed a penalty for underpaying his estimated taxes. The IRS stated that he was required to make payments equal to 90 percent of his current tax liability, or about $12,600. The agency demanded a $630 penalty for underpaying estimated taxes.

The man immediately wrote a letter to the service center that issued the bill. He pointed out that code section 6654(d) provides that "the lesser of" 90 percent of the current tax liability or 100 percent of the previous year's tax liability be paid through estimated payments. He attached a copy of his 1987 tax return to the letter. The return showed a 1987 tax liability of about $4,000. He also attached copies of Forms 1040 ES and canceled checks for the 1988 estimates, totaling about $5,700. With these facts, he proved that in excess of 100 percent of the 1987 liability was paid through estimates. As such, he complied with the statute. His final statement in the letter demanded an abatement of the penalty. The IRS obliged, abating a penalty in excess of $630.

90%100% Rule is Not Met. Earlier I stated that there is a defense in the statute that is very broad. The defense is found in section 6654(e)(3) and applies when you do not meet the 90%/100% rule. That subsection reads:

> (A) No addition to the tax shall be imposed under (6654) with respect to any underpayment to the extent the Secretary determines that by reason of casualty, disaster, or other unusual circumstances the imposition of such addition to tax would be against equity and good conscience.

This is the so-called "good conscience" defense. It applies when you can show that some type of disaster, such as fire, flood or "other unusual circumstances" prevented your making the correct estimated payments. This includes extensive medical bills, personal illness, injury or other events leaving you unable to manage your affairs or make the required payments.

The "good conscience" defense is very broad. It is undefined and unlimited, both in the statute and in the IRS' abatement guidelines. As such, the statute's lack of a definition of either an "unusual circumstance" or "good conscience" provides broad latitude to argue points and present facts that go beyond the boundaries of narrow definitions. Stated another way, I believe that we have a license to present everything but the kitchen sink (and maybe that too, if it caused a flood) as grounds for abating this penalty based upon the standard of "good conscience."

The Retired/Disabled Rule. The next defense in the statute applies to those who are retired or disabled. Section 6654(e)(3)(B) states:

No addition to tax shall be imposed under (6654) with respect to any underpayment if the Secretary determines that:

1. The taxpayer (I) retired after having attained the age of 62, or (II) became disabled, in the taxable year for which estimated payments were required to be made or in the taxable year preceding such taxable year, and such underpayment was due to reasonable cause and not willful neglect.

The "retired/disabled" test is narrower and clearly defined. If you have reached the age of sixty-two and retired during the year in question, or become disabled--either in the year in question or in the previous year--the penalty may be abated. In order to prevail, you must also show "reasonable cause" for the failure to make estimated payments. That is, you must show a causal link between the facts asserted as reasonable cause and the failure to make the estimated payments. The facts and circumstances alleged as reasonable cause must allow the reader to reach the conclusion that despite your effort to comply with the law, events beyond your control made compliance impossible.

Make Penalty Abatement Requests in Writing

Anytime you seek abatement or cancellation of a penalty asserted by the IRS, that request must be in writing. Your letter should clearly and with detail set out facts that allow the reader to conclude that you fall within one of the exceptions to the penalty being asserted. Where possible, provide documentation to support your claims. If, for example, you claim to have been injured or are the victim of a disaster, provide medical records or news reports to prove your claims. Send your letter to the IRS service center that issued the penalty and mail it via certified mail with return receipt requested. For more complete details on the penalty abatement process, please see chapter six of my book *41 Ways to Lick the IRS with a Postage Stamp*. It is an exhaustive discussion of the penalty abatement process as well as the appeals process applicable to penalties.

If Your W-4 is Altered

If you have done everything properly up to this point, including documenting the correctness of your W-4 at the time of filing it, you have next to no chance that the IRS will intervene in any way. You will enjoy withholding on the basis of the Form W-4 as submitted and you will "square up" with the IRS at the time of filing your return. You would have made the system work for you for a change, instead of you working for it.

But for claims that are not proper and cannot be documented, the IRS has the power to instruct an employer to disregard a Form W-4. In such a case, the agency instructs the employer on how to withhold. Generally, the instructions are to withhold on the basis of the most current previous W-4 submitted. Alternatively, the agency may instruct the employer to withhold on the basis of the agency's own determination as to the number of allowances you are entitled to claim. You may have claimed nine but the IRS believes you are entitled to eight. In that case, the employer is instructed to withhold on the basis of eight allowances.

In the worst case scenario, the IRS instructs the employer to disregard all W-4s and to withhold as though you were single claiming either one or zero allowances. In that case, about one half the paycheck is lost to wage withholding, though clearly the money is available in the form of a refund upon filing the tax return.

If you make a legitimate, provable claim, there is virtually no risk the IRS will instruct your employer to disregard your W-4. Those who run that risk are those who evidence tax protester behavior. These are people who have not filed tax returns for a number of years or who offer tax protester-type arguments as attachments to their W-4. Such arguments include claims that the tax laws, 1) are unconstitutional or voluntary, 2) that the laws do not apply to US citizens, or 3) that wages are not legally taxable as income. This list could go on but these are the main tax protester claims.

Even if the IRS were to tamper with your legitimate W-4, its direction to your employer is not final and you have the right to challenge the decision. The most simple and effective way of challenging the IRS' actions of improperly tampering with your W-4 is to contact the Taxpayer Advocate.

The Taxpayer Advocate

The Taxpayer Advocate is an office within the IRS whose function is to act as a liaison between the IRS and the citizen. Formerly known as the Problems Resolution Office, the Taxpayer Advocate has the authority to step in and order the IRS either to stop action it is taking or to take action it refuses to take. The Taxpayer Advocate has jurisdiction of a case when the IRS has or is about to violate the Internal Revenue Code or regulations, or where it is acting in a manner that will cause hardship to the citizen.

Provided your allowance claims are factually justifiable and within the law as explained in chapters two and three, the IRS has no legal right to order your employer to disregard your W-4. Should it do so, you may appeal to the Taxpayer Advocate for relief. The Taxpayer Advocate can direct the IRS to issue a letter to your employer explaining that your W-4 is proper and to recognize it.

To contact the Taxpayer Advocate, write a letter to your local IRS office, addressed to the attention of the Taxpayer Advocate. The letter should be mailed using certified mail, return receipt requested and should clearly and succinctly explain all the facts of the case. Provide a copy of the W-4, the IRS' letter of determination and all your worksheets showing how you arrived at your claim. Ask the Taxpayer Advocate to reverse the IRS' determination and order the agency to issue a letter to your employer explaining that your W-4 is proper.

I would never expect a W-4 case to get this far. However, we must recognize the fact that the IRS has been able to take advantage of people in the past because most simply do not understand their rights. When you are equipped to challenge IRS decisions, it is remarkable how reasonable the IRS can be. I provide more details and discussion on the Taxpayer Advocate in chapter seven of my book, *How to Get Tax Amnesty*.

CHAPTER FIVE
How to Double--Even Triple--Your Refund

I spent the first four chapters of this book making the case that you are committing a grave financial error allowing the IRS to hold your money. By now you should realize the significance of that statement. I also illustrated how, through a steady process of over-withholding, your refund is actually worth less than the face value of the check you receive from the US Treasury. But many of you may continue to cling to the idea of using the refund to save money. You may insist that while it is true that over-withholding may diminish the value of your refund, you have in fact managed to save money you otherwise would not have saved.

As I say in chapter one, if you use the withholding system to accommodate a spending spree every year, perhaps over-withholding is fine for you. But if you *really* do want to *save*, over-withholding is the world's *worst* way to do it. Even if you do not have the discipline to physically put the money aside--which is one reason over-withholding is attractive to so many--there are ways to work around that as well. As we move through chapter five, I expose you to several smart-tax strategies that show you how to double, triple--even more--the value of your refund in real terms as compared to what you receive from the IRS. What would you rather have, a refund worth $1,000 in real money, or one worth $3,000--or more?

Smart-Tax Ways to Save Money

Saving money is not a complicated process but a methodical one. By that I mean all that is necessary to save a lot of money over a long period of time is to repeatedly save a little bit of money over short periods of time. By doing that, you put the power of compound interest to work for you. I believe Einstein stated that the most powerful force in the universe is that of the power of compounding. It is compound interest that transforms a $100,000 home into a $300,000 expense requiring thirty years to pay.

Likewise, the Internal Revenue Service, using both compound interest and a staggering assortment of penalties, increases the average delinquent tax bill by about 270 percent. What begins as a difficult situation quickly mutates into an impossible one because of the power of compounding. So why not put the power of compounding to work for you? Up to this time, my guess is that far more people are harmed by the power than are helped by it. However, using your tax refund and the power of compounding to your advantage, you can save money and amass wealth much faster than you ever thought possible.

The following are seven Smart Tax Strategies to help you accomplish the goal of building wealth using nothing more than your $1,570 average annual income tax refund. After reading this, I believe that no reasonable person will ever again allow the IRS to handle his savings.

Smart Tax Strategy No. 1--A simple savings plan

Given the fact that your refund is reduced by an amount equal to the current year's withholding by the time you receive it, even stashing the money in a mattress is probably better than allowing the IRS to hold it. However, the mattress does not offer the power of compounding. Bank certificates of deposit do. By merely holding the money in a twelve-month certificate of deposit paying 6 percent annually, you begin immediately to grow the money, even from the first deposit of $130. At the end of the year, you saved $1,612.45. By the time you would normally receive your refund, you have another four or five months of $130 per-month investments in your possession--plus interest on that money.

You may argue that you would not have saved the $130 per month necessary to earn the interest in the first place. As mentioned more than once, too many people believe they do not have the discipline to actually save the money. That pitfall is easily avoided. Simply establish an automatic withdrawal arrangement with your bank. Have your bank automatically withdraw $130 per month from your account the same day that you deposit your paycheck. Have the money re-deposited into a savings account earmarked for a certificate of deposit after saving enough to buy the bank's minimum CD. Once locked into the CD, the money must remain there for the term of the CD or risk an interest penalty. Most importantly, the money is removed from your checking account and you cannot readily spend it.

It may be that $1,500 is not enough to purchase a bank CD. That is possible and each bank is likely to have differing requirements on minimum CD investments. Even if you cannot purchase a CD with just $1,500, you can open a simple savings account. And while a savings account interest rate is not as great as that paid by CDs, it is greater than that paid by the IRS. By having the bank automatically take your money each month (to guard against lack of discipline), it is just a matter of time before you have sufficient assets to move to the next level of saving or investment. The beauty is you steadily build wealth. Moreover, you do not have to wait until the usual tax refund date to begin. By adjusting your withholding, you can begin receiving your refund immediately at the rate of $130 per month. If you are six months into the year, you have $780 available with which to begin the plan.

Let us compare the real value of the tax refund using this strategy versus letting the IRS hold your money by examining the two charts on the next page. As you can see, even this simple strategy doubles the real value of your refund. Why allow the IRS to manage your money?

IRS-Managed Refund	Simple Savings Refund
Gross Refund $1,570 Less four months additional withholding (520) **Real value of refund = $1,050**	Gross Refund $1,570.00 Plus 6% interest over 12 months 42.45 Plus four additional months at $130 520.00 Plus interest on $520 25.24 **Real Value of Refund = $2,157.69**

Smart Tax Strategy No. 2--Managing credit card debt

Most Americans carry some credit card debt, whether it is from bankcards such as Visa or Mastercard or charge cards such as American Express or department store cards. We know that the level of consumer debt has exploded over the past several years and this is largely attributable to credit cards. The average person now has about $7,000 in personal credit card debt, not including car loans and home mortgages. Truly, we have become a debtor nation.

To make matters worse, personal interest such as that paid to credit card issuers, is not deductible. All interest must be paid with after-tax dollars. With a typical interest rate of 18 percent (and the power of compounding), credit card issuers get rich while the average person struggles just to keep his head above water. This is one area where you can make a big difference quickly in the real value of your tax refund. By using your tax refund to pay down credit card debt, it is equivalent to receiving a tax-free 18 percent return on an investment. At the same time, you do not run the risk of "spending" money each month because it is committed to paying down existing debt.

Use your $130 per month to increase the monthly payment against your credit card balances. If you have more than one card, use the entire $130 against the card with the lowest outstanding balance. Continue to make minimum payments against all other cards. When you sit down to figure your monthly bills, just add the $130 to the credit card payment. That way, the money is earmarked and not available for discretionary spending. The beauty is, each month you increase your net worth in real terms by paying down debt. While you are at it, make a similar commitment to stop using the credit cards for every purchase. If you have substantial credit card debt, I do not have to tell you how quickly the debts pile up. To really make an impact on your overall financial health, put the cards in a drawer or better yet, cut them in half.

Let us compare the real value of the tax refund using this strategy versus letting the IRS hold your money:

IRS-Managed Refund	Paying Down CC Debt	
Gross Refund $1,570	Gross Refund $1,570.00	
Less four	Interest saved	
months additional	at 18%	114.86
withholding (520)	Plus four additional	
	months at $130	520.00
	Interest saved on	
Real value of refund	$520 at 18%	106.50
= $1,050		
	Real Value of Refund	
	= $2,311.36	

Smart Tax Strategy No. 3--Building an insurance portfolio

Leaving an inheritance to your children is one of the best ways to provide for your family. Rather than lending the IRS $130 per month, why not use the money to build a life insurance portfolio? Whether you favor straight term insurance, annual renewable term or the purported investment features of a universal life policy, your money is much more valuable working for you than for the IRS.

Depending upon your age, a person can buy a substantial life insurance policy for $1,570 per year or $130 per month. At age forty, $130 per month buys a straight term policy worth about $1.4 million. For a policy guaranteed renewable for ten years, $130 per month gets you a death benefit of about $1.2 million. And $130 per month buys a universal life policy with a face value of about $225,000. Of the $130 per month premium, about $19.50 pays for the insurance and the remainder goes into building cash value. If you die while any of these policies is in effect, the $130 per month you were lending to the government instead provides you with a death benefit of up to $1.4 million, paid directly to your family.

Suppose you purchase a universal life policy for $130 per month with a death benefit of $225,000. You pay $19.50 per month for insurance and $110.50 per month goes into building cash value. You have the right to invest the overage each month into various mutual funds or money market accounts managed by the insurance company. Suppose further that through a combination of those mutual funds you were able to achieve a 12 percent growth this year--not unrealistic by any means. Through this strategy, you not only have the benefit of building wealth through making regular investments, but you put in place the means to provide for your family in the event of your untimely passing. Let us compare the real value of the tax refund using this strategy versus letting the IRS hold your money:

IRS-Managed Refund	Insurance Strategy	
	Gross amount to	
Gross refund $1,570	build cash value	$1,326.00
Less four	Capital growth	
months additional	at 12%	71.44
withholding (520)	Plus four additional	
	months at $110.50	442.00
	Four additional	
Real value of refund	months growth	60.13
= $1,050		
	Real value of refund =	
	$1,899.57	
	Plus Death Benefit of $225,000	

Smart Tax Strategy No. 4--Building an investment portfolio

Over the past five or six years, we have seen phenomenal growth in the stock market. We have seen so much growth, in fact, that borrowing money to invest in the market has become quite a passion. The number of margin accounts held with brokerage firms has grown by staggering numbers. Many people believe the market will just keep going. While I believe everything is cyclical and that what goes up must come down, there is little doubt that one should profit from the market while the cycle remains positive. The best part is you do not have to borrow money to do it and with the wide array of mutual fund investments available, you do not have to place your money at great risk.

However, for those willing to venture on the wild side with at least a portion of their holdings, it is certainly possible to get a 20 to 25 percent return on investment--or even more. Moreover, with the flexibility of today's brokerage accounts, you have the ability to move money from one investment to another at a moment's notice, whether it is stocks, bonds, hard assets, cash, etc. That way you can move into or out of stock investments depending upon the current market climate. By paying just a little bit of attention to the situation and utilizing the vast resources available to guide investors, it is quite easy to see how using this strategy can benefit you much better and faster than allowing the IRS to hold your money.

Let us compare the real value of the tax refund using this strategy versus letting the IRS hold your money:

IRS-Managed Refund	Stock Market Strategy	
	Gross Refund	$1,570.00
Gross Refund $1,570	Capital Growth	
Less four	at 25%	161.55
months additional	Plus four additional	
withholding (520)	months at $130	520.00
	Plus 25% on $520	148.53
Real value of refund		
= $1,050	**Real value of refund**	
	=$2,400.08	

Smart Tax Strategy No. 5--Fund a retirement plan

We know from the current economic statistics that the vast majority of citizens do not save money. If they did, the national savings rate could not be a negative number. Furthermore, citizens with cash in the bank should never pay 18 percent interest on credit cards or borrow home equity for every manner of expenditure. But that is exactly what happens today, despite the fact that the tax laws offer tax-deferred retirement savings plans which can build wealth relatively quickly.

If your company offers a 401(k) or similar retirement savings arrangement, you can use your $130 per month tax refund not only to begin an aggressive savings plan, but you can actually *increase* your take-home pay in the process. The following example illustrates how this is possible. Suppose your family gross income is $4,400 per month, which is about average. Suppose further that you are married and claim three allowances on your W-4. In addition, let us assume that you receive the average refund of about $1,570. Using the withholding tables in IRS Circular E, your withholding is $479 per month, making your net income $3,921 per month, exclusive of state income and social security taxes. (In the calculations to follow, we do not consider state income or social security taxes since neither is affected by Form W-4.) Given these facts, you are paying $479 per month in federal taxes but because of your refund, your liability is just $349 per month. You pay a $130 each month in federal income taxes you do not owe.

Generally speaking, employees not covered by company pension plans have the right to contribute up to $2,000 per year to an IRA. If your company has an employer-sponsored plan such as a 401(k), your contribution can be much greater. See chapter six for more details. Suppose you elect to contribute $1,570 to such an account. Watch what happens when you set this process in motion.

The first objective is to lower your withholding to an amount equal to your actual tax liability. Do this by adjusting your withholding to eliminate the refund as illustrated in chapter two. In examining Circular E, we see that as a general rule, adding four allowances to your W-4 reduces your withholding by about $130. (Be sure to consult the withholding tables that cover your specific facts.) Going from three allowances to seven gives you about $130 more per month in take-home pay. This means you are now paying only what you owe in federal income taxes--no more. You will not get a refund at the end of the year but you have $130 per month available to fund a retirement plan.

For purposes of figuring taxable income, IRA and 401(k) contributions are taken off the top. That is, money contributed to such accounts is not considered income. As a result, using the $130 per month to make an IRA contribution, your gross monthly income drops from $4,400 to $4,270 ($4,400 minus $130). You continue to receive $4,400 in gross pay but now, $130 is not taxed.

Using Circular E to determine withholding based on $4,270 of gross income and seven allowances, we find that your monthly withholding is $325. That means your net income is now $3,945 ($4,270 minus $325). That is $24 *more than* you were taking home at $4,400 per month gross. So, instead of getting a $1,570 income tax refund with no interest, you put the money to work in a tax-deferred savings plan. By the time you would normally receive your refund, you will have accumulated about $2,080 plus interest in your tax-deferred savings account.

What is more, you cut your overall income tax debt and put more money in your pocket in the process. This example put an extra $24 per month or $288 annually in your pocket--tax-free. It is just like finding money. To top it off, you have the option to re-invest the additional take-home pay into the IRA until you reach the maximum allowable contribution. If you do, the return on investment grows even larger.

In this example, the tables in Circular E made adjustments to withholding based upon an effective tax rate of about 18 percent. That means most of the income was taxed at 15 percent and some was taxed at 28 percent. If, in funding the IRA, you contributed money that would otherwise be taxed at the 28 percent level, the increase in your take-home pay is even greater. If you are in the 28 percent bracket, the same $130 per month added to an IRA puts $36.40 extra in your pocket each month.

There are still more savings to consider. If your state income tax rate is 5 percent, add another $6.50 to your increased take-home pay. Now you can see that your take-home pay could be as much as $45 more per month *after* you contribute $130 to the IRA as compared to allowing the IRS to hold your money for you. And do not forget to add the capital growth to the equation. Depending upon the nature of your investment, the growth could be as much as 20 to 30 percent on the entire principle amount over time.

To make matters even better, many employers offer a matching program to enhance the value of tax-deferred savings plans. Some companies do so at high rates, say dollar-for-dollar and some do so at lower rates. For example, say your employer matches your contribution at the rate of 25 percent. It means that for every dollar you invest, the employer invests an additional quarter on your behalf. The rate of matching depends entirely upon the employer but no matter what the rate, it is--in every sense of the word--*free* money. It is not money you would otherwise have earned and it is certainly not money that is taxed when paid. As long as it goes into the tax-deferred account, it stays there and is allowed to grow tax-free until you withdraw it later in life.

Shane is a young man who worked this plan exactly as outlined above. By placing the maximum allowable contribution in his company's 401(k), he actually increased his take-home pay by about $48 per month. He then invested that amount until he reached the maximum allowable contribution. The company matched his contributions at the rate of 50 percent. For every dollar he contributed, the company put an additional fifty cents into the pot. Shane invested the money into one of several mutual funds and assorted other investments. The money grew for over three years, at which time Shane decided he was ready to purchase his first home.

By the time Shane made the decision to buy the home, his 401(k) grew to just over $12,000 simply because he invested his refund as shown above as opposed to allowing the IRS to manage it for him. As it turned out, changes to the tax laws allowed him to take the money penalty free for the purchase of his first home. See chapter six. The power of compounding and tax savings combined to give Shane thousands of dollars in free money he never would have had if he continued the practice of allowing the IRS to manage his money for him.

In the above example, you can actually triple the value of the average refund. The increase in value is even greater for those in the upper income brackets. Let us compare the real value of the tax refund using this strategy versus letting the IRS hold your money:

IRS-Managed Refund		Retirement Fund Strategy	
Gross Refund	$1,570	Gross Refund	$1,570.00
Less four		Capital Growth	
months additional		at 25 percent	161.55
withholding	(520)	Plus four additional	
		months at $130	520.00
		Plus interest $520	148.53
Real value of refund		Federal and state	
= $1,050		tax savings	488.00
		Real value of refund	
		= $2,888.08	

Smart Tax Strategy No. 6--Fund a cafeteria plan or flexible spending arrangement

Childcare, insurance and medical costs are, besides taxes, three of the most pressing financial concerns for most Americans. Trying to find ways to pay for these things is a growing problem. While the expenses themselves grow, the ability to claim a deduction for them simultaneously shrinks. With more people filing short forms and congressional limitations on deductions in general, many families must pay these expenses with after-tax dollars. If you pay federal and state income taxes at the combined effective rate of 30 percent, you must earn $2,860 to pay $2,000 worth of medical expenses. An employer-provided cafeteria plan or flexible spending arrangement gives you the opportunity to pay these expenses with before-tax dollars using your tax refund to fund the plan.

A cafeteria plan is a benefit plan offered by a company to its employees. Under the cafeteria plan, employees can choose among several benefits, including accident or health insurance and reimbursement of medical bills. The plan is a means by which an employer can offer certain benefits to his employees with a double-bonus attached. The first bonus is the cost of the benefits is deductible to the employer. Secondly, the benefits are not considered income to the employee. Qualified benefits include group term life insurance, accident or health insurance for the worker and his family, dental insurance, actual medical costs, childcare assistance and legal expenses.

The flexible spending arrangement, or reimbursement account, is a program under which employees are reimbursed by their employers for health care costs not covered by insurance. The account can be funded either by employer contributions, a salary reduction agreement or a combination of both. Flexible spending arrangements are often operated under the umbrella of cafeteria plans.

Under a salary reduction agreement, your salary is reduced to pay for items the employer does not pay for. For example, suppose you pay $1,000 of medical insurance premiums. That amount can be paid for through salary reduction. In turn, the amount of salary reduction is not subject to income taxes. Another example would be medical bills not covered by insurance. This includes co-pays, deductibles or any other unreimbursed medical expenses.

The beauty of the salary reduction agreement is that you have the right to choose between the added salary or the benefit before beginning employment. This gives you the advantage of opting to pay accident or health insurance costs not otherwise paid for by the employer and the costs are paid for with pre-tax dollars.

Many employers offer these arrangements as fringe benefits to employees but not everybody takes advantage of them. First, many people do not fully understand these arrangements and because of the confusion, they opt not to participate. To clear up the confusion, we can simply state that these arrangements offer you the opportunity to pay for necessary living expenses with pre-tax, not after-tax dollars. Secondly, people believe they cannot afford these plans. However, by using your tax refund, you can fund such a plan and when you add a payroll deduction arrangement to the mix, the value grows substantially. In fact, by adjusting your withholding properly, you can actually end up with more take-home pay, just as you did in the previous example.

Keep in mind that benefits paid through a cafeteria plan or flexible spending arrangement are, like IRA or 401(k) contributions, taken off the top of your income. Thus, if you contribute $1,570 to such a plan, your gross income drops by that amount. By the time you are four months into the next year, you have contributed another $520 and you save about $488 in federal and state income taxes. Let us compare the real value of the tax refund using this strategy versus letting the IRS hold your money:

IRS-Managed Refund	Cafeteria Plan Strategy
Gross Refund $1,570 Less four months additional withholding (520) _____ **Real value of refund = $1,050**	Gross Refund $1,570.00 Plus four additional months at $130 520.00 Federal and state tax savings 488.00 _____ **Real value of refund = $2, 578**

Smart Tax Strategy No. 7--Pay down home mortgage debt

Though taxes consume more of the family budget than food, clothing, medical care and housing combined, there is no doubt that housing is a major family expense and one that is sometimes difficult to control. The reason is that interest rates, more so than any other single factor, dictate the cost of housing and we have no control over interest rates. Likewise, the example of housing provides us with the best illustration of both the positive and negative benefits of the power of compounding.

Earlier in this chapter I explained that the power of compounding is the reason a $100,000 house becomes a $300,000 expense over the thirty-year term of the loan. But why not turn that power to your advantage? Why not reverse, at least partially, the negative effects of compounding? If I told you that the value of your refund could be compounded up to six times its face value, would you hesitate for another moment to take advantage of that? I suspect reasonable people will not only take advantage of the opportunity, but will do so immediately.

Intellectually, we know that every dollar paid against a mortgage balance is one fewer dollar that incurs interest over the term of the mortgage. For example, if you paid one dollar more than your fixed payment with your first installment payment, the amount saved is equivalent to the interest charged on that dollar over the term of the loan. What few people understand is how profound the effect is upon the total cost of the loan over time. When the monthly payment is increased, even just a little--say $130--the savings are dramatic.

Let me illustrate this point using the example of a common mortgage. Let us assume you have an 8 percent, thirty-year mortgage on a $100,000 home and you are five years into your mortgage. By making *only one additional payment* of $130 in the fifth year of your mortgage, you cut $823--one month off the note. That is more than six times the return. If you do not believe me, boot up Microsoft Money or another similar computer program and figure it out for yourself. Certainly, you will be shocked at the outcome.

Now let us assume you make twelve extra payments of $130 each during the course of one year. This saves you $8,231 over the span of the mortgage--knocking one full year off the term of the note. Who would not invest $1,570 to get back $8,321? Ordinarily, this is called a "sucker bet," one that is clearly too good be to true. But in fact it is not because in the case of the home mortgage, you are on the hook for the principle amount of the loan and the debt accrues interest over the entire term of the loan--normally thirty years. Each dollar you pay against the debt cuts the interest. It is just that simple.

Next, let us suppose you pay $130 each and every month until the entire debt is paid off. First of all you should recognize that the $130 is not money down the drain. The $130 is the payment of principle. That is, every time you make such payment, you add equity to your home--your net worth increases. It is like putting money in the bank. Not only does your net worth increase, but over the period of the loan, you save $49,974--knocking ninety-five months off the mortgage. By using your tax refund in this manner, you turned a thirty-year mortgage into one lasting just over twenty-two years.

Let us now go to the next level of tax and financial management. By combining the strategy of building a retirement account and that of pre-paying mortgage debt, you can really build wealth quickly. Please refer to our discussion in Smart Tax Strategy No. 5. In that scenario, we invested the refund of $1,570 per month into an IRA or 401(k). We not only got the benefit of capital growth on the investments but cut the tax debt as well. The best part is, based upon the withholding tables set forth in Circular E, we actually increased take-home pay by $30.50 per month in that example. Watch what happens when the $30.50 is committed to pay down mortgage debt.

Assuming a $100,000 mortgage at 8 percent for thirty years, your payment is $733.76. By adding just $30.50 to the payment for one year--a total of $366--you save $3,401 in interest and knock five months off the mortgage. If you make the $30.50 payment every year for the term of the note, you save $27,436 in interest--knocking four years, two months off the note. Now which would you rather do, lend the IRS $1,570 interest-free or put the power of compounding to work for you in this dramatic fashion? Let us compare the real value of the tax refund using this strategy versus letting the IRS hold your money:

IRS-Managed Refund	
Gross Refund	$1,570
Less four months additional withholding	(520)
Real value of refund = $1,050	

Combined Retirement Fund and Mortgage Strategy	
Gross Refund	$1,570.00
Capital Growth at 25 percent	161.55
Plus four additional months at $130	520.00
Plus interest on $520	148.53
Federal and state tax savings	366.00
Interest saved	3,401.00
Real value of refund = $6,167.08	

Conclusion

By now it should be quite apparent that the tax refund is doing you no favors, especially if you really do want to save money. Instead, begin now to implement one or more of the above strategies and really begin to save--in big way!

CHAPTER SIX
How to Have More Than One IRA

Retirement planning has become a kind of national past time. Countless thousands of financial planners have grown up over the past two decades whose sole purpose is to help Americans plan for their golden years. The recent debates over the solvency of Social Security have heightened the awareness of the need for sound planning.

The Social Security program has been the cause of much concern for Congress and public policy advocates, and for good reason. At present, the program is on a collision course with financial disaster. According to a 1995 report of the president's Bipartisan Commission on Entitlement and Tax Reform, the growth of federal retirement and medical programs threatens to bankrupt the nation. The commission stated,

> The gap between Federal spending and revenues is growing rapidly. Absent policy changes, entitlement spending and interest on the national debt will consume almost all Federal revenues in the year 2010. By 2030, Federal revenues will not even cover entitlement spending.

The uncontrolled growth of federal programs and changing demographics of the US population work together to push the commission to a very sobering conclusion: "The current spending trend is unsustainable."

Not only is the spending trend unsustainable but with each passing year, it becomes less and less likely that Congress will be able to make good on its promises of retirement and medical subsidies under Social Security, Medicare and Medicaid. As of 1995, the liabilities of Social Security, Medicare, etc., were $17.4 trillion. Of those, $14.4 trillion are unfunded. That is to say, there is no money available to pay them. What is worse, the total assets of the programs, including "trust funds," were only $2.4 trillion. The reality is the money is just not there to pay the benefits Congress promised. That is why the commission repeatedly referred to the benefits package as a host of "unsustainable promises."

Since these revelations were made public in 1995, Congress and the president have done nothing to change the long-term outlook for Social Security. While much wrangling and debate has occurred, no substantive program changes have been acted. For this reason, no reasonable person can continue in the hope that Social Security and federal medical programs can provide the income necessary to sustain him comfortably in retirement. If you have not already begun to address this reality, now is the time. It begins with understanding the options available to help you build a retirement and health care plan.

Individual Retirement Accounts (IRA)

The one tax planning term we are all familiar with is "IRA," which stands for Individual Retirement Account. We have all heard of it and have a basic understanding of what it means. What many do not understand is the scope of flexibility you have with an IRA and the nature of the tax benefits that grow from it. Generally speaking, the IRA provides the following benefits:

- The employee gets a deduction for contributions made to the IRA for the year made;
- The fund set up to provide the retirement benefits is tax exempt;
- The employee is not taxed on his share of the benefits until they are distributed to him; and
- Certain lump-sum distributions receive favorable tax treatment.

In very general terms, the IRA allows you to invest money now and take a tax deduction for the amount contributed to the plan, up to certain limits. The general rule is that you may contribute up to $2,000 or the total of your taxable income, whichever is less. If you are an active participant in an employer-maintained retirement plan, the restrictions are greater.

Once invested, the money grows tax-deferred (not tax-free) until withdrawn. When the money is withdrawn, you pay ordinary income taxes on the amount taken in the year of the withdrawal. If you take a withdrawal before reaching age 59½, an excise tax--referred to as an early withdrawal penalty--of 10 percent of the amount withdrawn is added to the ordinary income tax. Thus, if you are in the 28 percent tax bracket when you take an early withdrawal, the penalty effectively taxes the withdrawal at 38 percent. Later in this chapter we explore several legal ways to avoid the penalty on early withdrawals. At this point, we examine the various ways to use your tax refund for IRA and other retirement plans that do not tempt you to just spend the money.

The 401(k). Many people think of the IRA and 401(k) synonymously but they are not the same. The IRA is an individual retirement account established by the employee to which he contributes his own money. For those with employer-provided retirement plans, the limitations on an IRA are severe.

The 401(k), on the other hand, is an employer-sponsored plan that gives the employee the option of deferring income. The deferred income is paid into a qualified retirement plan set up by the employer where it grows tax-deferred until the employee withdraws it. In addition, the employer may elect to match employee contributions, either dollar-for-dollar or on some other basis. Neither employer nor employee contributions are taxed until withdrawn by the employee.

The 401(k) is not subject to the same $2,000 limitation as is the IRA. Rather, under a 401(k), you may elect to defer up to $10,000 to a 401(k)--five times that of the normal IRA.

The spousal IRA. Earlier I stated that an IRA contribution is limited to either $2,000 or the total of gross income, whichever is less. Because of this limitation, many non-working spouses believe they cannot contribute to an IRA. But that is not true. Section 219(c) of the code expressly provides for a spousal IRA for married couples who file joint tax returns.

Under the rules for spousal IRAs, each spouse may make a deductible contribution to a separate IRA of up to $2,000, even if one has little or no income. The only proviso is that the combined gross income for both spouses (even if only one earns income) equals or exceeds the amount contributed. For example, suppose one spouse earns $45,000 per year and the other spouse earns nothing. Each spouse may contribute up to $2,000 to an IRA since the total contribution--$4,000--is less than the total combined gross income of $45,000. If either spouse is an active participant to an employer-sponsored retirement plan, there are limitations to the amount that may be contributed.

By using the spousal IRA provisions of the code, a family can actually double what is otherwise the maximum amount it may contribute to an IRA. Use your tax refund to fund an IRA or begin making contributions to your company's 401(k) plan.

Self-employed plans. Self-employed persons may also set up and establish their own IRAs that face some of the same limitations as those utilized by employees. However, self-employed people have additional options that can greatly increase the amount they can contribute. The first option is a so-called SIMPLE retirement plan. The second option is the so-called SEP-IRA. I address each in turn.

SIMPLE stands for "savings incentive match plan for employees." Any employer without another retirement plan and who has fewer than 100 employees can start a SIMPLE plan. To participate, the employees must have received at least $5,000 of compensation during the previous tax year. For purposes of this plan, the employer is considered an employee. Thus, if the self-employed person is the only employee, a SIMPLE plan may be established provided his earnings were more than $5,000.

Under the SIMPLE plan, the employee may contribute up to $6,000 to the plan even though the normal limit for IRA contributions is $2,000. In addition, the employer can match the contribution up to $6,000. This means a total of $12,000 annually can be contributed to a SIMPLE plan.

The beauty of this plan is that the employee himself can give up to three times the normal IRA contribution. But when the employee is also the employer, as in the case of the self-employed, the maximum contribution is $12,000--six times that of the typical IRA. Moreover, because one half of the total contribution is actually an "employer" contribution, that portion is deductible from the self-employed person's Schedule C gross income. As such, you do not pay self-employment tax on the employer-contributed funds. That is a savings of 15.3 percent in addition to the federal and state income tax savings.

The second option is the so-called "simplified employee pension" plan or SEP. This plan is much like the SIMPLE plan but offers greater capacity for deductible contributions. Under the SEP arrangement, one contributes to an already established IRA. The contribution may be the lesser of $30,000 or 15 percent of the employee's compensation. Again, for purposes of this plan, the self-employed person is considered an employee.

The amount contributed under the SEP does not come from the employee's salary the way a normal IRA or 401(k) contribution does. Rather, the amount comes from the employer's funds. As such, the amount contributed is a business expense deduction for the employer. As such, when the self-employed person is also the employee for whom the contribution is made, this has the effect of reducing the employer's Social Security tax bite. For this reason, when the employer contributes to a SEP on his own behalf, the tax savings are nearly twice that of a contribution to a normal IRA. Moreover, because of the increased limits of the contribution, a self-employed person may contribute substantially more to his SEP than to a traditional IRA.

The Roth IRA. The Roth IRA is the latest in the series of retirement planning devices created by Congress. The Roth IRA is a hybrid arrangement under which one makes *non-deductible* contributions to an IRA. In exchange for paying tax on the contribution now, the citizen is allowed to take tax-free distributions in the future of both the principle investment and its earnings. In other words, while there is no deduction for the amount contributed to the Roth IRA, there is likewise no tax liability on the distributions taken from it.

The maximum amount one can contribute to the Roth IRA is $2,000. Just as with the traditional IRA, both husband and wife may contribute up to $2,000 each, even if just one spouse earns income. However, the total gross income must be greater than the sum of the two contributions.

In order to be considered a tax-free distribution, a Roth IRA withdrawal must meet certain rules. First, it cannot be made within five years beginning with the first taxable year for which the contribution was made. Assuming the five-year rule is met, the distribution is not subject to tax if it is made:

- on or after you reach age 59½;
- to your beneficiary or to your estate on or after your death;
- after you become disabled; or
- for first-time homebuyer expenses for you or your spouse or children, grandchildren and ancestors.

When it came into effect, many people used the conversion capability of the Roth IRA to switch their traditional IRA to a Roth. By doing so, they were able to take a penalty-free distribution from the traditional IRA provided they rolled it into the Roth IRA. However, by making the conversion, they incurred ordinary income taxes on the full amount of the traditional IRA. The theory was that given Roth's feature of no tax liability under the above rules, what was lost in taxes by making the conversion now would more than be made up with completely tax-free accumulations in the future.

Maybe that is true and maybe it is not. It depends upon many things, not the least of which is your capacity to grow the money while it is invested. Certainly the decision to convert should not be made without carefully analyzing all the facts in consultation with a qualified and experienced financial planner. Regardless of whether it is beneficial to convert existing IRAs to a Roth, it very well may be beneficial to hold both a traditional IRA and a Roth. The law allows you to have both but the total annual contributions to both cannot exceed $2,000. Use your tax refund to fund the plan.

The Medical Savings Account

The Health Insurance Portability and Accountability Act passed in August of 1996 created a program known as the Medical Savings Account (MSA). Code section 220. The MSA is available to anyone who is either self-employed or the employee of a "small business." A small business is defined as a business with fifty or fewer employees. The MSA must be used in conjunction with a "high deductible" insurance policy. It cannot replace insurance or be used to purchase insurance. The insurance must be in place in order to enjoy the MSA.

The MSA acts much like an IRA. You create an MSA through an independent trustee just as with an IRA. MSA contributions are tax deductible, just as with an IRA. However, there is a great difference between the two. Withdrawals from the IRA are taxable but not from the MSA. When you make a payment for medical expenses not covered by insurance, you *are not* taxed on the distribution. This gives you an effective 100 percent deduction for the medical expense even if it does not exceed 7.5 percent of adjusted gross income.

Furthermore, there is no "use it or lose it" rule as with some fringe benefit programs offered by employers. For example, under the flexible spending arrangement we discussed in the previous chapter, if you do not spend what is in the account, you lose the money. However, money in the MSA grows if you do not spend it and is available for future expenses in later years.

Annual contributions to the MSA are limited. Individuals may contribute up to 65 percent of your insurance deductible. Families may contribute up to 75 percent. If the money is taken for non-medical purposes, a 15 percent penalty applies in addition to the normal tax rate. The penalty does not apply if you are over 65 or in the case of death or disability. You may roll funds from one MSA to another within sixty days of withdrawal and not incur the penalty.

The MSA is a valuable tool for many Americans because the restriction on itemized deductions for medical expenses means that most people have few expenses they can deduct. To be deductible on the Schedule A, the medical expense must exceed 7.5 percent of adjusted gross income. At that, the average family with, say $50,000 of adjusted gross income, cannot deduct the first $3,750 of medical expenses each year. But with the MSA, you can contribute a fixed amount to a medical fund each year. The money can be invested and grows until you need it for expenses not covered by insurance. When the money is used for medical expenses that would otherwise be deductible on Schedule A but for the 7.5 percent limitation, there is no tax on the withdrawal. This gives you the best of both worlds: a deduction on the front end of the contribution but no tax on the back end of the distribution. Use your tax refund to fund an MSA.

The Education IRA

Another of the recent changes Congress made to the savings environment is the addition of the education IRA. This is a tool that allows parents to set money aside for the higher education of their children. Annual contributions of up to $500 per dependent may be made by parents to a trust account much like an IRA. The money grows tax-free during the period it is held in the education IRA. Provided it is used for qualified higher education expenses, the money is not taxed even upon distribution.

Higher education expenses include tuition, fees, books, supplies, equipment, room and board required for enrollment or attendance at an educational institution. If the qualified higher education expenses of the student are equal to or more than the amount taken from the education IRA, then all of the earnings are considered tax-free. If the qualified higher education expenses of the student are less than the amount taken from the education IRA, the excess is taxable. In addition, a 10 percent penalty applies to such distributions.

You should note that the $500 annual contribution to an education IRA is not deductible. However, the distribution of the principal amount is not taxed in any event. Provided the money is used for the education of the dependent, the earnings are likewise not taxed.

You can make a $500 annual contribution per child and there is no limit to the number of children involved provided that they are your dependents. They must be under age eighteen. In addition, transfers and rollovers can be made from one education IRA to another with no tax consequences. Not only can the money be moved from one account to another but can be moved from beneficiary to beneficiary. Suppose for example, you have three children for whom you have been making $500 annual contributions. Suppose the oldest child elects to go into the military rather than pursue college. At that point, you can split the money in his education IRA between the two remaining children with no tax consequences.

Penalty-Free Distributions from Retirement Accounts

Normally, if you take a distribution from a retirement account before reaching the allowable age, you face not only the ordinary income tax on that distribution but a 10 percent penalty for early withdrawal. Unlike other penalties in the tax code, this penalty is not subject to cancellation because it is, in reality, another tax. The additional tax is added to the ordinary tax as an incentive to keep the money invested until you reach the authorized distribution age, usually 59½.

The tax code provides several circumstances under which a distribution may be taken free of the penalty. Under no conditions is a distribution free of income tax. Let us explore the various circumstances under which one may take a distribution free of the penalty for early withdrawal under code section 72(t).

Medical expenses. The penalty does not apply when the distribution is taken to pay medical expenses, however the amount withdrawn cannot exceed the amount allowable as a medical deduction. This provision is available whether or not you itemize deductions during the year in which the expenses are paid.

IRS Levy of IRA. With the IRS Restructuring Act, the penalty does not apply to a withdrawal if it is caused by the IRS actually levying the IRA for payment of delinquent taxes. In that case, the withdrawal is considered income in the year of the levy but there is no penalty for early withdrawal.

Medical insurance during unemployment. If a person has been unemployed for at least twelve consecutive weeks and has received state or federal unemployment benefits during that time, he may take a penalty-free distribution to pay for medical insurance. This exception does not apply once you become re-employed for a period of sixty days. If you are self-employed and not entitled to unemployment compensation, you may nevertheless take the distribution penalty-free if you would have otherwise qualified for unemployment compensation.

Higher education expenses. A penalty-free withdrawal can be taken to pay for higher education expenses. The expenses must be incurred during the year of the withdrawal and the withdrawal cannot exceed the amount of the education expenses. The expenses can be for yourself, your spouse, your children or grandchildren of either yourself or your spouse.

First-time homebuyer. Penalty-free distributions can be taken to pay for the costs associated with the purchase of your first home. The home must be your principal residence and the costs must be paid within 120 days of the distribution. This exclusion applies not only to a home you purchase but also to that of your spouse or any child, grandchild or ancestor of you or your spouse. The exclusion applies to the costs of acquiring, constructing or reconstructing a residence and includes any usual or reasonable settlement, financing or other closing costs. A $10,000 cap applies to this provision.

Double-check exclusions. Because the tax law is always changing and Congress regularly adds and deletes benefits from the tax code you should always check with your retirement plan administrator before taking any distribution to determine whether it will be considered a penalty-free withdrawal. The last thing you want is to be surprised by a 10 percent penalty you did not see coming.

The Self-Directed IRA

Anyone invested in a retirement program of any kind is aware of the mind-numbing array of investment alternatives available. Among them are more than 7,000 mutual funds offering stocks, bonds, currency, international investments, money markets and countless other holdings. In addition are the many thousands of individual stocks and other holdings traded on the various exchanges throughout the nation and world. In the final analysis, there are limitless investment alternatives.

Given this universe of products, it seems hard to believe that holding a traditional IRA may pose some limitations but it is true. In order to hold assets in a qualified retirement plan, the assets cannot be held by you, the investor. A qualified trustee must hold them in trust for you. This is where the limitation arises.

Many banks, brokerage houses and mutual fund companies are generally qualified to act as trustee on retirement accounts. However, they are willing to do so only for their own products. For example, Oppenheimer investment company is happy to establish an IRA on your behalf and to function as the trustee on the account. However, you must be invested in one of its mutual fund products before it will do so. This is fine if you do not intend to diversify out of Oppenheimer products. The minute you do, you must find another trustee to hold the new asset and that trustee often presents the same limitation.

Now, suppose you wish to purchase the stock of a single company and hold it in your IRA. Stocks, such as blue chip corporate stocks, are usually not handled by large investment companies such as Oppenheimer. They must be purchased through an independent broker. The problem is that independent brokers are generally not qualified to hold assets in trust for IRA purposes.

Each time you establish a new IRA with a different management company, there is an initial fee. It may be just a few dollars or as much as $100. Each year there is a fee to manage your assets. Again, this may be very small or more significant. In either event, if you have more than one account, your fees start to add up. Add this to the limitation expressed above and you begin to see problems with the typical IRA.

The solution to the problems of cost and efficiency in maintaining several IRAs is to establish your IRA through an independent trustee. This arrangement is known as a self-directed IRA. An independent trustee is distinguished from an institutional trustee in this important fashion. The institutional trustee generally acts as trustee only over the assets that it sells. On the other hand, the independent trustee functions as trustee over any asset that can be legitimately held by an IRA. This includes any mutual fund, money market account, individual stock issue, bonds, CDs, savings account, etc.

How to Find an Independent Trustee. Independent trustees generally take the form of one of two types of company. The first is a bank and the second is a trust company whose primary function is to manage investment assets. There are two ways to track down companies in your area that can do the job.

1. State Regulatory Authorities. Each state has a banking commission that regulates its state banks. It also has an authority that regulates public trust companies. In some states, they may be one in the same agency. These agencies are able to tell you who in the state has the authority to function as an independent trustee for your IRA. Obtain the names and addresses of several banks and trust companies, then interview them using the guidelines outlined below. You may wish to begin your search by contacting your Secretary of State. That office can tell you specifically which state agency is responsible for oversight and can give you names and phone numbers of contacts within those agencies. The Secretary of State may already have a comprehensive list of approved trustees.

2. Federal Regulatory Authorities. All national banks and national trust companies are regulated by the Comptroller of the Currency, a federal office located in Washington, DC. A phone call to the Comptroller of the Currency in Washington can produce a list of national banks and trust companies approved to function as independent trustees for IRA purposes.

How to Choose a Trustee. Take care when choosing an independent trustee. After all, you are entrusting your retirement assets to the care of this company. However, please understand this trustee is merely the custodian of your IRA. You are the director of the account. That is to say, you have total control over the assets the account invests in, the period of the investment and the investment ratio. This is what makes for a "self-directed" IRA. You steer your own investment ship.

It is this control feature that helps to significantly reduce your investment risk. You choose the investment vehicle and how the assets are to be held or managed. Even the most conservative investor can limit risk by holding assets in CDs or similar vehicles. The trustee does not and cannot execute any trades that you do not specifically authorize. On the other hand, the trustee makes no warranty concerning the nature of the transactions you direct. The trustee's function is to carry out your investment wishes while holding the assets in trust in accordance with section 408 of the tax code. With regard to the integrity of the specific investment, you are on your own but that is the case with your present IRA. If the investment goes bad, your capital is reduced.

Questions to ask your potential independent trustee. The following are questions to ask and points to be aware of while interviewing potential independent trustees.

1. History of the company; how long in business, etc.
2. What are the fees charged for services performed. Obtain a clear and concise statement of all fees and charges, including annual fees and fees for individual transactions. Compare these with other companies in the area to see if they are reasonable.
3. Who regulates the company? Find out specifically which state and federal agencies are responsible for oversight of their activities. Then, follow up with those agencies. Find out if there have been any specific problems or complaints with regard to their fiduciary duties. If so, get the details.
4. Ascertain the procedure for making trades. Look for simple procedures allowing you to make the trades you desire. At the same time, there should be some kind of security procedure in effect to safeguard your account so others cannot trade your holdings without your knowledge or consent.

5. Ascertain the procedure in effect to determine ownership of the assets held by the trustee. The assets held by the trustee do not belong to the trustee. In the event of some kind of financial problem involving the company or another of its clients, you want assurance that your assets are clearly identified as your assets and not commingled with others.

6. Ask for references from investors who have dealt with the company.

7. Ask for broker references. Brokers are the entities from whom one purchases the investment products held by your IRA, such as stocks, bonds, etc. The trustee deals directly with brokers in executing your investment wishes. Brokers can give you some insight into the reliability of the various candidates for the job.

8. Ask for a copy of the trust company's most recent audit report. All trust companies are audited regularly by outside accounting firms. Check the "Exceptions" page of the report. It discloses any problems.

9. When investing in stocks and bonds, be sure your assets are segregated and not commingled with the holdings of other investors. Find out how the assets are titled. They should be held thusly: "In trust for (your name)," or "For the benefit of (your name)." You should also find out where the securities are held, i.e., in what physical location.

Gold and Silver--a Major Advantage. One major advantage of the self-directed IRA is the ability to invest in gold and silver coins. Generally, collectibles are not permitted to be held by an IRA. However, an exception to that rule is expressed in code section 408(m)(3). That section allows gold and silver "eagle" coins issued by the United States under 31 USC section 5112(a) and (e) to be held by an IRA. The same law allows coins issued by any state, as well as gold, silver, platinum or palladium bullion to be held in an IRA.

This gives great investment latitude to the self-directed IRA and offers a decided advantage to the small investor. By putting a portion of your assets in gold and silver--hard money-- you are protected from the potential of ravaging inflation or falling currency values.

Such coins can be purchased in a number of ways. Generally speaking, the institutional IRA trustees do not sell them because they did not create the product. As a result, the self-directed IRA is about the only way to hold gold or silver coins in your IRA.

Before establishing a self-directed IRA, do your research carefully. Weigh the factors outlined above, especially the cost and desire to invest in assets not offered through an institutional management company.

Working with Financial Advisors

This chapter is by no means exhaustive on the topics addressed. It is intended to acquaint you with the various types of programs available and how they might benefit you in your situation. Before acting on the ideas expressed here, you are well-advised to consult with a financial advisor with the skill and experience necessary to answer questions about your specific situation. Act only after you have the background and information necessary to guide you.

CHAPTER SEVEN

Smart Tax Strategies to Cut Taxes for the Self-employed and Wage Earners

All this talk about reducing tax liabilities for the employee must have the self-employed wondering, "Hey! What about me?" Anyone who has operated his own business knows the self-employed take a pounding but the news is not all bad. In this chapter, we examine some of the smart tax things a self-employed person can do to reduce the bite. In addition, we look at even more strategies the wage earner can employ to cut his tax and double his refund.

Tax Smart Ways to Spend Money

Managing a small business is a major challenge. Today, it is not good enough to make the best widget in the world. It is not good enough that your widget costs 30 percent less than your competition. It is not good enough that you can perform a service in half the time and at half the cost of others. In short, it is not good enough to be the best at what you do.

To survive in small business today, you must have money management savvy. You must have at least basic knowledge of tax law and procedure, the political climate, current business trends and an ability to see future trends. You must realize that business comes in spurts. One year runs in the red and the next is a record-breaker. Lack of such savvy is one reason so many businesses are just a flash in the pan.

Perhaps the most critical element of the success of a small business is timing. When is the right time to advertise? When is the right time to spend money on new equipment or to hire more people? When is the right time to cut back inventory? When is the right time to develop new products? When is the right time to pay bills? When is the right time to save money? Timing is everything.

Because taxes are so much a part of your small business, I submit that the right time to spend money is the time when you can realize the most tax advantages. Whether your method of accounting is the cash basis or accrual basis, prepaying expenses at the right time provides thousands of dollars in additional deductible expenses you may otherwise pass up. Prepaying expenses is especially advantageous when your business had an exceptionally profitable year. This could apply to independent contractors, salesmen, sole proprietors or any corporation, large or small. In millions of cases, this smart tax spending trick can provide an escape from a very serious tax trap.

The trap I refer to is the penalty for failure to make estimated tax payments properly. Each year, well over five million business people are penalized for failure to make proper estimated tax payments. So, while our smart tax spending tricks may seem basic and simple to implement, they are tricks millions of people just do not use. The trap is set when large chunks of unexpected revenue come in. Let me give you an example. Let us say Jerry, the insurance salesman, finally closes the big commercial account he worked on for years. Prior to landing this account, Jerry earned about $50,000 per year, after expenses. Considering a mortgage, a couple of dependents and other deductions, his taxable income was $30,000. For a married couple filing a joint return, the federal tax liability on this income is figured at 15 percent for federal and 15.3 percent for self-employment taxes. This amounts to a combined federal tax bill of $9,090.

However, income from the new account added $30,000 to Jerry's taxable income and it all came in November. It appears Jerry's tax liability doubled overnight. But it is much worse than that. Only about $8,000 of this new income is taxed at 15 percent. The remaining $22,000 of increased income is taxed at the higher rate of 28 percent. All of it is subject to the 15.3 percent rate for self-employment taxes. Consequently, the federal tax liability is now $21,040. Even if Jerry immediately pays the difference of $11,950, it appears he has failed to make his estimated payments properly. You can see how Jerry's windfall suddenly becomes a curse.

What should Jerry do? Let us examine his business a little. In the insurance industry, the largest commissions come in the first year a product is sold. They get smaller as policies are renewed. Since renewal of Jerry's large account produces substantially less income next year, Jerry expects once again to be in the 15 percent tax bracket. Since Jerry expects to be back in a lower tax bracket next year, he should consider every option available to do two things. One, lower his taxable income this year, when his income is high. And two, reduce his expenses next year, when his income drops to more normal levels.

Every dollar by which Jerry lowers his income this year saves as much as sixty cents in federal, state and self-employment taxes, not to mention penalties. Here are some smart tax spending tricks Jerry or anyone like him can use to accomplish the two goals mentioned above. Remember, in order for these smart tax spending tricks to be effective, Jerry has to act before December 31.

Prepay business expenses. Every business has normal recurring expenses including:

- Auto lease
- Equipment lease
- Utilities, including phone, heat and electric
- Postage
- UPS and other shipping charges
- Cleaning expenses
- Subscription fees
- Employee insurance fees
- License fees
- Office Rents, and
- Other miscellaneous expenses.

Why not prepay some of these expenses in the year the income is high? If, in our example, Jerry pays these expenses in the year of his windfall, the tax benefit is about twice what it would be if he waits until the following year. In addition, he has the added benefit of going into the following year with a number of his regularly occurring expenses already paid. This provides the bonus of not having to pay such expenses in a year when he knows his income will be down. That helps him to weather any potential unforeseen financial storm that may be on the horizon.

There is an additional bonus to using this technique. That is the ability to negotiate discounts with suppliers or vendors when prepaying expenses. Suppose you are considering prepaying office rent. First contact your landlord. Discuss your plans and seek a concession in exchange for the prepayment. For example, the landlord may be willing to give a five percent discount on your rent if you prepay by six months. Now you have earned three benefits by prepaying. First, you pay deductible expenses in a year when income is high. Second, you go into the next year with some operating expenses paid at a time when income is expected to drop. Third, you save money on the expense by negotiating a reduction in cost in exchange for prepaying. Now that is tax smart!

Add to a retirement account. Another important technique to reduce income in a high-profit year is to add to a tax-deferred retirement account. If Jerry has not yet opened a retirement account, now is the time to do it. The contribution Uncle Sam effectively makes will likely never be as great as it is in the high-income year. In effect, it costs Jerry only about $40 out of his pocket for every $100 he puts in his retirement account. See chapter six.

Prepay personal deductible expenses. Jerry should consider prepaying as many deductible personal expenses as he can. These include property taxes, state income taxes, charitable contributions, etc. I provide more details on this topic later in this chapter. This is a strategy that can also benefit the ordinary wage earner as explained more thoroughly later.

Prepaying personal itemized deductions can actually lead to more deductions than you are otherwise entitled to. Let me explain. Suppose you are married and file a joint return. Before it pays to itemize deductions, they must exceed the standard deduction. The standard deduction for married filing jointly is $5,000. Code section 63(c). Suppose your normal itemized deductions equal $7,500 per year. By prepaying $4,000 of certain expenses, you push them to $11,500 in a given year. However, since these deductions were prepaid in one year, they cannot be claimed the next year. As a result, your itemized deductions for the next year fall by $4,000, to just $3,500. Now it pays to claim the standard deduction of $5,000, rather than itemized deductions of $3,500. By doing this, you actually *increase* your total deductions over two years by $1,500.

How did that happen? Ordinarily, you would have claimed $15,000 in deductions over the two years; $7,500 per year. By prepaying $4,000 in deductions the first year, you end up claiming a total of $11,500 in itemized deductions in one year and $5,000 in standard deductions the next year for a total of $16,500. If you pay taxes at the effective rate of 36 percent, this technique saves you $540.

Whether or not your business experiences a windfall, these smart tax spending tricks can help reduce the burden. In many cases, it requires no extra income or cash flow to accelerate the payment of certain expenses. Paying some bills even a few days early--say December 27 instead of January 3--can provide hundreds, even thousands of dollars in extra write-offs for the small business.

Use Your Insurance Policy to Turn $5,000 into $10,000 Overnight

Whether you are a W-2 wage earner with an existing retirement plan, a W-2 wage earner without an existing retirement plan through your employer or you are self-employed, I think you will be surprised to learn of the options available using the cash value of your life insurance policy and your tax-deferred retirement plan.

Before we begin this discussion, please recall the caveat I issued at the end of the previous chapter regarding retirement plans. The laws in this area are complex and change often. Anytime you set out to establish or deposit money into a retirement account, be sure to consult a retirement planning expert who can evaluate all the facts and circumstances of your case. It simply is not a good idea to make a move in this area without sound guidance.

Having said that, let us address the question of how the cash value of one's life insurance policy can be used to multiply your wealth. Let us say you have $2,000 cash value in a life insurance policy you can borrow at 5 percent. The first question to ask is, can you get better than a 5 percent return on the money elsewhere? In the market environment of the late 1990s, the answer surely is yes. Suppose you find an investment paying 15 percent.

Now assume your tax liability for the current year has been paid in full, either through wage withholding or estimated tax payments. Further assume the tax is computed without regard to any IRA or retirement plan deduction. (For the sake of simplicity, I use the term IRA to describe all retirement plans during the course of this discussion.) The law gives you until April 15 of the year following the tax year in question to contribute to an IRA. That is, IRA contributions deductible in 1999 can be made up until April 15, 2000. Therefore, by making the contribution, you have the potential of getting a refund of taxes already paid. Let us walk through a simple scenario.

Suppose you pay combined federal and state income taxes at the effective rate of 36 percent. Remember, all taxes have been paid through wage withholding. By placing $2,000 (or the limit of your deductible amount) into an IRA, you create a $720 refund to which you were not otherwise entitled. That is the amount of *refund* you are entitled to when you increase your deductions by $2,000 as a result of the contribution. To figure the amount of refund you receive, simply multiply the amount of your contribution by your effective tax rate. In this example, a $2,000 contribution x 36 percent equals a $720 refund.

Of course, by borrowing the insurance money at 5 percent, you created an obligation to pay interest on the loan. Therefore, considering current taxes of 36 percent, you must earn at least 7.9 percent on the $2,000 to cover the interest obligation. If you earn more than 7.9% on your investment, you have successfully created positive cash flow--however small it may be--from nothing.

There are two ways to deal with the earnings from the IRA. Ideally, you should allow those earnings to remain under the tax-deferred umbrella of the IRA. This allows them to continue to grow and prevents application of the early withdrawal penalty. Even though you may leave those earnings in the IRA, you nevertheless have a positive cash flow position if your return is at least 7.9 percent (in this example).

The second alternative is to take the earnings from the IRA investment and use the proceeds to service the loan obligation. However, when you take current earnings from an IRA or similar retirement vehicle, you face not only the income tax, but also a 10 percent penalty for early withdrawal of the funds. Therefore, to cover the early withdrawal penalty, your return must increase by at least 10 percent. Instead of 7.9 percent, you would have to earn 8.7 percent on the $2,000 invested (in this example).

Now, what do you do with the $720 tax refund windfall? Here are some options:

- Spend the $720, knowing your long-term financial goals are still intact.
- Use the money to repay a portion of the loan you took to make the investment. This reduces your monthly interest payment obligation and increases the amount of positive cash flow you have created. In the case of a $2,000 loan, you will cut the size of the loan by more than one-third.
- Invest the $720 into your IRA. If you are limited to a $2,000 contribution in one year, wait until the next year to make the deposit. By electing this option, you really get the benefit of the multiplying effect of the strategy, particularly in light of the fact that earnings on the $720 will grow tax-deferred over the time of the investment.

Let us examine what happens when you re-invest the $720 refund into your IRA. First, you earn another tax deduction. Again, assuming you pay tax at an effective rate of 36 percent (28 percent federal and 8 percent state), you get an additional refund of $259.20. If you invest that, you get another $93.31 refund. By re-investing all of the refunds, you end up with more than $3,120 in your IRA, instead of the original $2,000 in cash value in the insurance policy. You increased your earning power by more than 50% and the investment grows tax-deferred over time.

The Potential Risks. One obvious risk is if you find yourself in a financial jam and need the money in your IRA to live or pay bills, you face the 10 percent penalty for early withdrawal. Assuming you are in the same tax bracket when you withdraw the money as when you invested it, you pay 36 percent in taxes and another 10 percent in penalties. A total of 46 percent of your distribution is lost.

Another risk is that tax rates could rise by the time you take your money out. Unless federal spending is brought under control, you can count on lawmakers to rely on tax increases alone to address deficit problems. History bears this out. There are investments that hedge against the kind of risk created by irresponsible government spending. Precious metals are among those investments. When financial times get bad, metals seem to be the investment safe haven of choice. As we discussed in the previous chapter, it is possible to hold precious metals in your IRA.

A third risk is that you may make a bad investment. This is an inherent aspect of investing. Some ideas on how to minimize that risk are discussed in the previous chapter under the heading "The Self-directed IRA." You should also consider relying upon the guidance of a trusted and experienced investment counselor to minimize risk.

If you do have some financial trouble in the future, you may well be in a *lower* tax bracket when you need the money. Dropping from the 28 percent federal bracket to 15 percent means you pay 13 percent less in federal taxes. This more than compensates for the 10 percent penalty.

Higher Tax Rates--Lower Risk. Obviously, the higher the tax rate you pay, the lower your risk in any tax-deferred retirement plan. The highly compensated may well find themselves in the highest federal tax bracket of 39.6 percent. Considering other factors such as deduction phase-outs, state income taxes and loss of exemptions, you could easily find yourself losing up to half of your income to taxes. With this in mind, any investment is less risky when the IRS--in effect--makes a contribution to your retirement. I shall illustrate this point.

Our previous example used $2,000 as the amount borrowed from a life insurance policy to invest into an IRA account. But employees with 401(k) plans and the self-employed are often allowed to deposit more to their retirement plans. Whether and to what extent you can make deductible contributions should be settled between you and your employer or investment advisor.

For the sake of illustration, let us assume a self-employed person can make a deductible investment of $5,000 into a tax-deferred retirement account. Let us also assume that person pays taxes at the effective rate of 51 percent (federal, state and social security taxes), and that all current tax liabilities are paid. A $5,000 deposit results in a $2,550 refund. By investing the refund, you earn another $1,275 refund, and so on. By reinvesting all tax refunds, you turn a $5,000 investment into more than $10,200, virtually overnight.

Maximizing a Wage earner's Benefit. I have not forgotten wage earners who participate in an employer-sponsored retirement program. You too can use the cash value in your life insurance policy to increase your investment potential. Contributions to a company-sponsored 401(k) are usually withheld from the employee's paycheck. In many cases, the employee does not make the maximum contribution because he needs the money to provide daily living expenses. In that case, borrow the cash value of your life insurance to make a deductible contribution. Be sure the reduced tax liability offsets the obligation to service the loan while increasing your retirement fund balance.

If you have a policy that is nine or ten years old, there may be another option. Some policies reach a point where premium payments must no longer be made to keep the policy in force. Policy earnings provide enough money to cover the minimum premium while leaving your death benefit intact. If this is the case, consider converting your monthly insurance premium into deposits into your retirement account, up to the deductible limit.

Tax Time Trouble-Shooting. Each year, more than 3.5 million citizens find themselves short of money when it comes time to pay taxes. These citizens face penalties for late payment and failure to make timely estimated payments. If you find yourself in this predicament, your life insurance policy may be of great value.

As stated earlier, IRA investments can be made up to April 15 of the year following the tax year in question. Contributions for 1999 may be made until April 15, 2000. Suppose on April 10, 1999, you discover you owe $1,000 in federal taxes. If you do not pay the tax by the 15th, you are subjected to the penalty for failure to make adequate estimated payments. Total penalty and interest assessments could double the amount owed.

If you file the return without the money, collection notices begin arriving within several weeks. Even an automatic extension of time to file the return, IRS Form 4868, does not help since it does not give you additional time to pay the tax. Thus, penalties and interest continue to mount on the unpaid portion of your tax.

The cash value of a life insurance policy may provide the funds necessary to make an IRA contribution before April 15. Under this circumstance, it is possible that a contribution will return a far better investment than anything discussed so far. In this example, $2,000 transferred from the insurance policy to a tax-deferred retirement account cuts your tax liability by $720 (assuming an effective tax rate of 36 percent). Now, instead of facing a $1,000 tax bill, your bill is just $280. More importantly, however, what you save in penalties and interest matches the tax savings and keeps you out of trouble with the IRS.

It should be noted that despite IRS denials, it is possible to win an extension of time to pay your taxes. To do so, use Form 1127, *Application for Extension of Time to Pay Tax*. File it by the due date of the tax, usually April 15. The application is not automatic. However, if granted, you receive up to six additional months to pay the tax without penalties. Interest does run on the unpaid tax, however. For details on how to file Form 1127, please see *41 Ways to Lick the IRS*, pages 217-221.

How to Double Your Property Tax Deduction

Whether you are self-employed or a wage earner, if you own a home, you can profit from this smart tax strategy. The reason is every homeowner pays real estate taxes each year to local government. Using this strategy, you can double your property tax deduction in a given year. That way, you can use the higher deduction to offset unexpected income or to give yourself a greater tax refund.

Most people pay their property taxes one year behind. For example, in May of 1999, Minnesota homeowners pay one-half of the property taxes assessed in 1998. In October of 1999, the second half of 1998 taxes is paid. Most states function in a similar manner. To double your property tax deduction for one year, pay the 1999 property taxes by December 30, 1999, rather than during the next year. The result is your property tax deduction for tax year 1999 doubles. I will explain.

Assume your annual real estate tax bill is $1,500. Your mortgage company paid property taxes in 1999 (for taxes assessed in 1998) with money from your escrow account. This fact earns a deduction of $1,500. If you pay property taxes by the end of 1999 that are normally due in 2000, you will have paid another $1,500 during the 1999 tax year. Because all taxes were paid in 1999, you are entitled to a real estate tax deduction of $3,000. Most people are entitled to claim deductible expenses in the year the expense is paid. It rarely pays to put off paying expenses until the next year. Pay as many deductible expenses as possible in December. That way, they are deductible on the tax return for that year.

To insure proper credit when pre-paying taxes, follow these simple step-by-step instructions.

1. Mail your payment via certified mail, return receipt requested, about the middle of December. It is best if the tax department receives your payment before the end of the year. Mail the payment to the county tax assessor or other official responsible to collect real estate taxes. If you are unsure who this official is, call your county courthouse and ask questions.

2. Include a letter that clearly indicates you are paying taxes due the following year. Be sure to note the property identification number (PIN), address of the property and other identifying information on your letter as well as on your check to insure proper credit.

3. Audit-proof the claim. Be sure to obtain a receipt from the county. Make a copy of it and include it with your tax return at the time of filing. Include IRS Form 8275 to make full disclosure to the IRS of your deduction. You may raise some eyebrows at the IRS when you suddenly show a deduction twice the size of your usual claim. However, by audit-proofing the claim, you avoid having your return selected for audit. For more details on audit-proofing, please see the final chapter of this book.

Before prepaying any expense, consider the impact on your net tax liability. Obviously, if the additional tax deduction does not lower your net tax liability, do not prepay the expense. Save this smart tax spending trick for a time when it will help.

Some may not have the extra money by the end of the year to prepay these taxes. For those who escrow tax payments, there may be hidden cash available to make the payment. The cash is in the form of the balance of your escrow account held by the mortgage company. By prepaying the tax, you relieve the mortgage company of the obligation. This should entitle you to a refund of the real estate tax component of the escrow account.

After making the prepayment, notify your mortgage company of your action. Write a letter explaining what you did and include a copy of your receipt from the county. Ask the mortgage company to refund the money specifically set aside to pay property taxes. The mortgage company cannot refuse when you provide proof of payment.

The amount of money available in your escrow account depends upon a number of factors. You may have an amount equal to your prepayment. If so, you have effectively prepaid your taxes and doubled your property tax deduction *without* incurring any additional financial burden. Check the escrow balance before you make a prepayment. Then, limit the prepayment to an amount equal to the tax escrow balance. That way, the money you get back after prepaying the tax is equal to the amount of the prepayment itself. This ensures you do not have to go into your pocket for cash to increase your property tax deduction.

You can also pay the full tax then get a refund over time. Consider the fact that each time you make a mortgage payment, additional funds are escrowed for taxes. So even though the money in your escrow account at the end of the year may not cover the full prepayment, the escrow account builds each month. In Minnesota, property taxes are generally due in May and October. Therefore, enough money to pay your tax obligations would have to be in escrow at those times. Time your refund claim to correspond with the normal due date of the tax payment. This ensures that sufficient funds are available to repay you.

Whether your escrow balance covers all or part of a prepayment, you are assured that your escrow fund will never have more money in it than you actually need to cover pending liabilities. Your money will always be working for you, rather than for the mortgage company. Remember though, once you start the process of prepayment, you must continue the habit. Failure to prepay next year could result in a loss of one year's worth of property tax deduction. However, as explained earlier, that fact could still work to your advantage by claiming the standard deduction.

This strategy is not limited to those who escrow their real estate tax payments. It can apply to those who have income windfalls as well. Let us consider a few examples. Suppose you are about to retire from a high paying executive position. Presently, your effective tax rate is 50 percent, after combining federal, state local taxes. Upon retirement, your effective rate drops to 22 percent. The difference between the two is 28 percent.

By prepaying property taxes in the high tax year, you receive an effective tax-free return on the investment equal to the difference between the two tax rates. Even a 10 percent reduction in your tax bracket provides the equivalent of a 10 percent tax-free return on investment for any amount of money used to prepay property taxes.

Another common scenario involves the impending retiree. Upon retirement, many individuals receive a one-time lump sum payment as severance pay, a buy-out or other retirement fund distribution. A lump sum payment of $100,000, for example, would surely move one to an effective tax rate of 50 percent. Fully half of the distribution could be lost to taxes. But because the payment is a one-time distribution, the citizen drops back into a much lower tax bracket the next year. The tax leaves him with substantially less money on which to live in the future years, when his income is back to normal levels.

Such a person should consider prepaying property taxes. Unlike income taxes, property taxes do not decrease in proportion to your income. If anything, they increase. By prepaying property taxes in the year of the large distribution, you not only reduce the effective rate of tax on the distribution itself, but you minimize your living expenses in future years when your income has once again dropped to normal levels.

Now let us consider the insurance salesman, like Jerry, who had an extraordinarily great year. Suppose he earned $30,000 more in 1999 than he did the year before. The windfall, however, will not repeat itself and he knows the 2000 earnings will be back to normal. In anticipation of the drop in income for 2000, Jerry may choose to prepay tax deductible expenses in the year of plenty. In that way, he both reduces his tax burden at a time when income is high and reduces his living expenses at a time when income is low.

How to Increase Your State Income Tax Deduction by 25 Percent or More

This is a smart tax strategy especially useful for the self-employed. The self-employed must pay estimated taxes on a quarterly basis. Generally, the state issues payment coupons you must send in by the date indicated on the stub itself.

In most states, the fourth quarter payment is due January 15 of the following year. State income taxes are deductible on your federal income tax return in the year paid. Therefore, payments you make after the tax year ends *are not* deductible in that tax year. For example, the payment made on January 15, 2000, for 1999, is not deductible in 1999. A full year must go by before you get the benefit of the write-off.

In order to increase your state income tax deduction by up to 25 percent, you need only make the fourth payment a couple of weeks early. That is, make the payment in December not January. Be sure to send your payment via certified mail, with return receipt requested. To ensure proper credit, use the payment coupon provided by the state and be sure to note on your check the tax year to which the payment applies. Mail the check in time for your state revenue department to post the payment before the end of the year.

Please note most people are entitled to claim a deduction in the year the expense is paid. Even if the creditor does not cash the check until the next year, as can be the case with year-end payments, you are entitled to claim the expense in the year you wrote the check. IRS often misleads taxpayers by referring to the date of payment as day the check was paid by your bank. However, the rule is different. The payment is considered made when you lose constructive use of the funds. That happens the day you write your check, not the day the check is paid by your bank. More on this in the last two chapters of this book.

There are ways to use this simply strategy to stay out of trouble. Usually when state estimated income taxes are due, federal estimated taxes are due as well. Each year, millions of citizens are short of money at the time they are to make their final estimated tax payments. The knee-jerk reaction to not having all the money is to pay just the IRS. If you find yourself short of money to make both estimated payments, consider paying the state first.

Assume at year-end you owe $3,000 in taxes. You owe the IRS $2,000 and the state $1,000. You have just $2,000. Let us examine what happens if you pay the entire IRS bill but ignore the state liability for the time being. First, by failing to pay the state by year-end, you lose $1,000 worth of deductions you could have claimed on your federal return. If you are in the 28 percent federal tax bracket, you effectively increased your federal liability by $280. As a result, the $2,000 payment is not enough to cover the federal liability. You may face a penalty for underpayment, in addition to the state tax bill. Even without regard to penalties, you are now a total of $1,280 short of money needed to pay all taxes.

A better option is to pay the $1,000 you owe the state and send the IRS the other $1,000. Now, you are only in the hole by $1,000. By paying the state, you eliminated $280 of federal tax liability and the potential state penalty.

Now let us take the strategy one step further. By paying the entire $2,000 to the state, you *decrease* your federal liability by $560 ($2,000 x 28%). As a result, you now owe the IRS just $1,440. Next, file your state return immediately (as soon after January 1 as possible) to get back the $1,000 you overpaid. If you act quickly enough, you can get the state refund in time to send it to the IRS by April 15. In addition, you now must come up with only $440 additional by April 15 to pay the IRS.

If you do not have the money to pay your tax in full when due, you have at least limited the amount of the shortfall and ultimately, the penalty. By paying the state all of your available funds, you reduced your final tax liability from $1,280 and two penalties to $720 and one penalty. That is a swing in your favor of $560 and one penalty. In addition, since the shortfall is reduced rather dramatically by simply paying the state first, your chances of paying the entire balance due by April 15 are increased. This, in turn, can save even more penalties.

Those who experience an unusual increase in income one year may find themselves in a dramatically higher tax bracket. When this happens, consider prepaying state income taxes. This operates to reduce your tax bill in the high-income year while limiting expenses in the low-income year. This option is available to you whether you are self-employed or a wage earner. If you are a wage earner, you can increase your state income tax payments in one of two ways.

First, have more state income tax withheld from your check. Second, make a separate payment to your department of revenue before the end of the year. As always, send your payment via certified mail, with return receipt requested. Write your social security number on the check and be sure to indicate the tax year to which the payment is to be applied.

Please note, anytime you get into the habit of prepaying taxes, you have to continue in order to avoid losing deductions. If you prepay state taxes one year but fail the next, you cut your deduction in the next year by 25 percent.

How to Double One Month of Your Mortgage Interest Deduction

The technique for doubling one month of your mortgage interest deduction epitomizes common sense money management. The process is really quite simple. As is the case with many deductions, the date of December 31 is significant.

Most mortgage payments are due around the first of each month. To double one month's worth of your mortgage interest deduction, simply pay your January payment a few days early. If you pay the January payment by December 31, the interest included in the January payment becomes deductible in the prior year. As a result, you end up with thirteen month's worth of mortgage interest paid over a twelve-month period. You have doubled one month's worth of the deduction and increased by 8 percent your overall mortgage interest deduction. You do it without increasing your payments.

A word of caution is very important here. The tax law does not allow a deduction for *prepayment* of interest expenses. The average citizen can take a deduction for interest only in the year the interest *accrues*, even if paid early. Code section

461(g)(1). It is important to understand the strategy outlined here does not involve *prepaying* interest.

If your mortgage payment is due on the first of the month, your payment includes interest that accrued during the previous thirty days. Thus, your January 1 mortgage payment includes interest that accrued against your account during the month of December. When you pay the interest in December, you are entitled to claim the deduction in December. However, most people do not pay the January payment until January. That means they cannot claim the deduction until the next year.

What if your payment is not due until the 15th? In that case, your payment includes interest that accrued partially during the previous month and partially during the current month. You can still accelerate the payment but the deduction is smaller. The following illustration shows how to figure it.

Since December has thirty-one days, the January 15 payment includes sixteen days worth of interest that accrued in December. To figure your deduction for sixteen days of interest, start with the total interest included in your monthly payment. Suppose the interest portion of your payment is $600. Divide $600 by thirty-one days to find the daily interest assessment. In this example, the result is $19.35 ($600 / 31). Now, multiply the daily interest charge by the number of days interest accrued in December. In this example, the result is $309.60 ($19.35 x 16). The amount of $309.60 is the additional interest you can deduct when you pay your January 15 payment by December 31.

This is a one-time increase in the mortgage interest deduction. You must now continue in this habit each year to avoid losing one monthgs worth of deductions the next year. For example, if you do not accelerate the payment in the next year, you end up with just eleven month's worth of the deduction. If there is no financial benefit to accelerating this deduction, save this strategy for some time in the future. Perhaps next year you will make more money and the added deduction has more value. Also remember to compute the effect of the standard deduction after accelerating itemized deductions. You may end up with a larger slice of the overall pie.

To accelerate the deduction, simply send the January payment early. Ideally, send it in time for the mortgage company to *receive* it before the end of the year. This ensures the information return issued to the IRS by your mortgage company reflects the total interest paid throughout the year, including your accelerated payment.

It is also a good idea to send a letter along with your payment instructing the mortgage company to include the extra interest in the year in question. Remind them that the IRS considers the date of payment to be the date in which you gave up constructive use of your money. You will recall from our earlier discussion that this occurs on the date you write the check, not on the date the recipient cashes it or the date your bank pays it.

If the mortgage company does not acknowledge this payment on the information return filed with the IRS, claim the extra deduction anyway. Provide an affidavit with your return to explain to the IRS the reason for claiming a higher interest deduction than is indicated by the mortgage company. Audit-proof the claim as outlined in chapter ten of this book.

Given the nature of the mortgage interest deduction, other opportunities to accelerate mortgage interest may be available. For example, if you purchased your car with a home equity loan, accelerating your car payment may give you another one-time tax deduction. The payment only need be made a few days early to make this happen. The same is true for boats, motorcycles, snowmobiles, a computer and even a color TV. Any extra interest payment you make on anything you used a home equity loan to buy is tax deductible, *provided* the interest already accrued as explained above.

How to Claim the Home Office Deduction

Many small businesses simply cannot be profitable if they must rent commercial office space. For one thing, those pursuing part time self-employment endeavors simply do not need commercial office space to develop their undertaking. These people should consider establishing a home office.

The problem with pursuing this option is the fact that there is so much confusion over whether one's home office is deductible. Thankfully, Congress passed a law in 1997 that helps to simplify the issue.

The legal basis of the deduction. The deduction for the home office grows from code section 280A(c). That provision allows a deduction for the costs connected with maintaining an office which is, a) "the principal place of business for any trade or business of the taxpayer," b) is "used by patients, clients, or customers in meeting or dealing with the taxpayer in the normal course of his trade or business," or c) is "a separate structure which is not attached to the dwelling unit," and is used in connection with your business.

Here we find the basis of the home office deduction and the conditions that must be met. First, the office space must be used regularly and exclusively for business purposes. The exclusive use test is very important. The space in your home office must be used *only* (not most of the time) for business purposes. If your home office doubles as a TV room during evening hours, you do not meet the exclusive use test.

If you do not meet that test, you get no deduction whatsoever. That is, you cannot allocate the percentage of personal use versus business use and take a deduction equal to the percentage. The exclusive use test is an all or nothing standard. If there is any personal use, you do not qualify for the deduction. Therefore, the area of your home used for business should, ideally, be segregated from the remainder of the home. A separate room, such as a spare bedroom, is ideal. If you use a portion of your basement, the best solution is to wall off the office area with bookcases or file cabinets to create the office space.

Under code section 280A(c)(1)(C), you are entitled to a deduction if your office or business space is a separate "structure not attached to the dwelling unit." If you have converted a garage or built a separate building to accommodate your business, you are clearly entitled to deduct the costs associated with that building. As long as you meet the exclusive use test, nothing more need be proved to win the deduction.

Under code section 280A(c)(1)(B), you are entitled to the deduction if the space in your home is used "by patients, clients, or customers in meeting or dealing with the taxpayer in the normal course of his trade or business." The statute makes it clear that if you regularly meet with business associates in your home office, you may claim the deduction. In fact, the single best way to avoid problems with any home office claim is to be sure that you do in fact have such meetings. If you do not presently conduct meetings in your home office, arrange your affairs so as to meet with clients, customers or patients on a regular basis.

If you do not have a separate structure or do not meet regularly with clients or customers in your home office, you must meet the "principle place of business" test set out in section 280A(c)(1)(A) of the code. That section provides that your home office must be your "principle place of business" in order to qualify.

What is the "principal place of business?" For tax years beginning with 1999, the phrase "principal place of business" includes a location used for administrative or management activities of any trade or business if there is no other fixed location of that business. That is, if your home office is the only location of your business and you use that space for bookkeeping, customer contacts, paper work, etc., your home office qualifies as a principal place of business. This is true even if you spend a substantial amount of time working elsewhere, such as a traveling salesman or construction contractor.

If you do conduct administrative or management activities at another location, you still qualify if those activities are not substantial. For most people whose only office location is within their home, they will qualify.

In 1991, the IRS created Form 8829, *Expenses for Business Use of Your Home*. That form is a separate itemization of all expenses claimed for the use of a home office. It must be filed with your tax return whenever claiming a home office deduction. The form also helps to determine whether any of the deduction limitations apply to you.

Home Office Equipment. Even if you cannot claim a deduction for any costs associated with maintaining a home office, the equipment you place in your home office remains deductible as long as it is used for business purposes. Telephones placed in your home office, the fax or copy machine, file cabinets, desks, etc., are all items that can be claimed as legitimate business expenses in the year purchased, provided they are legitimately used for business purposes.

If your equipment is used partially for business and partially for personal use, then determine the percentage of business use and claim a corresponding deduction. If your desk is used 50 percent for business and 50 percent for personal use, claim 50 percent of the cost of the desk as a deduction in the year purchased.

Increase Deductible Business Expenses

For businesses, the key to paying fewer taxes is to claim more legitimate deductions. One way to do that is to increase your deduction for business tools and equipment. Tools and equipment needed to carry out your business are considered capital assets. Ordinarily, investments in capital assets cannot be deducted. Instead, they must be depreciated over the useful life of the item.

For example, suppose you purchase tools for use in a construction business. The IRS takes the position that because those tools can be used over several years, their costs cannot be fully deducted in the year of the purchase. Rather, the cost must be spread over the life of the tools. If the useful life of the tools is three years, you may claim one-third of the cost in each of three years, beginning with the year of the purchase. The requirement to depreciate makes it more difficult to recover your costs and increases your tax debt.

One section of the tax code, however, gives you an option that can save a lot of money. It is code section 179. In essence, code section 179 states that a person can elect to expense items in the year of purchase rather than depreciate them over their useful life. The election must be made on Form 4562, *Depreciation and Amortization*, at the time of filing your tax return. Once the election is made, you are stuck with the results.

My question is why would anybody choose to depreciate property if they have the option of taking a full deduction for its cost in the year of the purchase? Clearly, by claiming a full deduction in the year of the purchase, you cut your tax significantly. One answer to the question is that there are limits on how much property can be expensed under section 179. For tax year 1999, the maximum amount deductible is $19,000. Any property over that amount must be depreciated. For tax year 2000, the amount is $20,000; for the years 2001 and 2002, the cap is $24,000; and for the years thereafter, the cap is $25,000.

Another important limit to the section 179 deduction applies to "listed property." If your business property falls into this category, you must meet a business use test in order to enjoy a section 179 deduction. Listed property consists of the following:

- Any passenger automobile or any other property used for transportation;
- Any property which is ordinarily used for entertainment, recreation or amusement including photographic, communication and video-recording equipment;
- Any computer and related peripheral equipment; and
- Any cellular telephone or similar telecommunication equipment.

If your company purchases listed property, you cannot claim the section 179 deduction unless the property is used more than 50 percent of the time in connection with the business. For example, if you purchase a personal computer that is used one-third of the time in a home business and two-thirds of the time for non-business purposes, you cannot expense the computer under section 179.

This is not to say you cannot claim a deduction for the business-use portion of the computer. However, you must depreciate the business-use portion over the life of the computer. Say for example you spend $1,500 on a computer that is used one-third of the time in your business. This gives you a business expense of $500 ($1,500 / 3). You claim the $500 as a depreciation deduction over the life of the computer, which we will say is three years. At that rate, your depreciation deduction is $167 ($500 / 3). The depreciation begins in the year the property is placed in service.

There are more special rules and limits for passenger automobiles. For tax year 1999, the section 179 deduction is limited to $5,000; for the year 2000, the limit is $2,950 and for years thereafter, the cap is $1,775. You must reduce these limits further if the business-use of the car is less than 100 percent.

When claiming a section 179 deduction for listed property, be sure to keep adequate records of how the property is used so you can prove that it is used more than 50 percent in your business. See chapter nine for more details on record keeping.

Cut Costs by Using Independent Contractors

Employees can cost a fortune. For most small businesses, it is not wages, salaries or benefits that cost the most. The bigger problem is expenses of withholding for federal and state income tax and social security tax purposes, the multitude of accounting requirements for reporting pension and other benefits, federal and state unemployment taxes and workers compensation costs. The taxes alone for a given worker can, in some states, amount to 20 percent of wages paid. That is, the taxes paid on five workers could pay the salary of a sixth employee.

One way to avoid these growing costs and administrative burdens is to use independent contractors for your service needs. An independent contractor is nothing more than a self-employed person who provides goods or services to other businesses. Because the contractor is self-employed, your business does not bear the costs associated with employees. You need not withhold on payments made to him and you need not account for him in connection with other non-tax federal employment regulations.

You should know that there is nothing illegal or improper about using independent contractors *legitimately*. A legitimate contractor is not an employee masquerading as a self-employed person. A legitimate contractor is a person who is truly self-employed. He operates his own business. He makes his services available to the general public or other businesses. He owns his own tools and maintains his own office. He probably advertises his business. And he probably does work for a number of other clients. He works on his own time, subject only to the terms of contracts he negotiates. That contract is usually in writing. He can hire and fire his own employees. In the final analysis, he can gain or lose on a given contract, depending upon his own actions. He files a tax return using Schedule C reporting his income and expenses from his self-employment activity.

On the other hand, the improper contractor is really someone's employee. The employee must report to work at a given time. He works only for a wage, salary or commission. He does not control the work place or the manner in which the work is performed. He does not advertise his services to others and does not work for others. He owns no equipment of his own and all work is done using his employer's equipment. He has no office of his own. He cannot hire others to do the work for him. In the final analysis, he cannot lose in a given situation because he is paid a salary or wage. Even if the business owner loses money in a given transaction, the employee still gets paid his wage.

Do you see the difference between an independent contractor and an employee? To boil it down to a simple formula, it is this: who has the right to control (whether or not that power is used) the work place, including tools and equipment, the worker and the manner in which the work is performed? If the worker controls those things, he is self-employed. He is a legitimate independent contractor. If the employer controls those things, the worker is his employee.

Mike was a small jewelry manufacturer who fell on hard times. He had a goldsmith who worked for him as his employee. Brian reported to work and used Mike's tools and equipment in Mike's small factory to make jewelry for Mike's customers. Mike had a salesman in the office and a clerk.

When Mike's business sank, he had to cut overhead drastically. He cut the size of his space in half then laid off the clerk and the salesman. That cut his payroll and rent but it also left him without adequate space to manufacture his jewelry. He also faced Brian's payroll each week. To satisfy the space and payroll problem, Brian went into business for himself.

Mike sold Brian a workbench and a wide assortment of the tools. Brian set up shop in the basement of his own home. He paid the phone bill, utility bills and all other expenses associated with running the shop. Mike and Brian negotiated a rate at which Brian would be paid to make various items. Mike brought orders to Brian who manufactured them in his home shop. Brian collected fees for his services and Mike in turn sold the finished pieces to customers.

Brian--not Mike--controlled the work place and manner in which the work was performed. Brian controlled his own hours. His only obligation was to deliver a finished piece within a pre-stated time that met certain specifications. Brian had the right to hire others to do the work. Almost immediately, Brian circulated his name among other jewelers in town, making his services available to them. In fact, on many occasions, Mike referred business to Brian. Brian stood to gain or lose on every deal he made. If he spent too much time on a project, messed up the setting or broke a diamond, he would have to bear the cost. In every sense of the word, Brian was self-employed.

Mike was able to stay in business at greatly reduced cost. After Brian became a contractor, Mike was left with no employees. He completely eliminated the costs of withholding, matching taxes, accounting, quarterly payments and employment taxes returns, together with all the hassles that accompany those burdens.

Not every business can legitimately eliminate all employees and go to contractors. But most businesses can use contractors in place of some employees. To the extent that your business functions can be performed by contractors, consider doing this as a legitimate cost saving device.

If you use contractors, it is a good idea to:

- Use a written contract to specify the nature of the relationship, and spell out the critical elements of control. The contractor must have control as outlined above;
- Be sure the contractor uses his own tools and equipment. If he uses your tools and equipment, he should pay a fee for their use;
- Be sure the contractor pays his own insurance where applicable;

- Be sure the contractor *understands the relationship* and his obligations. Provide written notice of the fact that he is obligated to report his earnings on a tax return and pay self-employed taxes;

- Be sure you report to the IRS on Form 1099 the earnings paid to the contractor. If the earnings are less than $600 per year, you have no legal obligation to report but do it anyway. It shows good faith and could be an important step in avoiding potential penalties. See *Taxpayers' Ultimate Defense Manual*, Chapter Six, for more.

- Be sure you make no effort to disguise your employees as illegitimate contractors. It will not work and could cost you a fortune in back taxes and penalties.

Conclusion

How much will these three smart tax techniques save you each year? Ever dollar in taxes you save is one more dollar you have available to hire more workers, expand your facilities, obtain more equipment, do more marketing and in general, make your business and family life more productive and enjoyable. Controlling your tax bite is the first step toward putting your business and life on the fast track to success.

CHAPTER EIGHT
All But Forgotten Deductions

Many people are under the impression that tax breaks are only for the rich. The perception is, if you are rich, you get a tax break. The truth is, if you get a tax break, you can become rich. Let me prove it.

According to IRS Publication 1136, *Statistics of Income Bulletin*, the top one percent of income earners--those earning more than $200,000 per year--pay about 25 percent of all individual income taxes. This is true even though they earn only about 15 percent of all taxable income. The top 5 percent--those earning more than $100,000 annually--pay over 55 percent of all income taxes. The fact is, the rich pay through the nose.

Now that you can see the rich do not receive all the tax breaks, let me also prove that getting tax breaks can make you rich. Let us examine what just $1,000 in extra tax deductions could mean to you each year. Assuming you are the average person with average income, an extra $1,000 per year in tax deductions can:

- Knock $49,000 of interest off your home loan over the term of a thirty-year mortgage;
- Get you $2,000 worth of luxury options on the new car you buy every five years;
- Add $5,000 to your savings account earning just 6 percent over ten years;
- Buy $50,000 worth of universal life insurance if you are age thirty-five or younger; or

- Grow to $15,000 in a tax-deferred retirement account in just fifteen years.

Now imagine what $2,000, $3,000 or even $5,000 per year in extra tax deductions can do for your financial picture. The problem is that too many people just give up on deductions, believing they are not worth the hassle. That is one reason why so many people--now close to 70 percent of all citizens--file the short form.

Tax deductions are not just for the rich. In fact, they can benefit you--the average citizen--more so than the rich because you can probably less afford to pay your taxes. With this in mind, let us explore several deductions you might not know are available. If you did know, you may believe it not worth the time or hassle to claim them. Please do not forget how profound an additional $1,000 per year in tax deductions can be to your financial picture.

Deduct This Book

Most realize their tax return preparation fees are deductible but did you realize the cost of educating yourself on the tax law is deductible? Code section 212(3) allows a deduction for any of three categories of tax-related expenses. They are those associated with:

- The determination of any tax liability;
- The collection of any tax liability; and
- The refund of any tax already paid.

The purchase of material to help in the determination of your tax bill, such as this book, is a tax-deductible expense. Similarly, money you spend to defend yourself in connection with the collection of taxes, such as for books to help with audit defense, is a tax deduction under code section 212(3). As a result of that code section, any material you purchase from Winning Publications is a tax-deductible expense. See the ordering information at the end of this book.

Businesses claim the deduction as a business expense. Individuals claim it as a miscellaneous expense on Schedule A. To be deductible, miscellaneous deductions must exceed two percent of adjusted gross income. Because of this limitation, too many people overlook them. However, after considering all the deductions we discuss, you will likely find it worth the time to claim the benefit.

Educational Expenses

Do you spend money on education to keep pace in your job? Did you know that most educational expenses are deductible? Code section 162 provides that educational expenses are deductible when the education is:

- To improve or maintain a skill required in your job or by your employer or by your trade or business; and
- Required by your employer or by law or regulation, to maintain your employment, status or rate of pay.

You must already be employed or self-employed to deduct educational expenses. Educational expenses are not deductible if:

- The education is the minimum required to qualify you for a job; or
- Qualifies you for a new job, trade or business.

It is important to note, however, that once you meet the initial qualifications for a particular job, trade or business, additional educational expenses are deductible, even if they improve your skills to the point where you realize a change of duties. A change of duties is not a new job, trade or business if it involves the same general work.

Consider the example of a teacher. If she takes classes allowing her to step up to teaching high school from grade school, the education did not result in a new trade or business. She is still a teacher though at a higher level. She is entitled to deduct the costs of her education.

The deduction includes the expenses for unreimbursed items needed for the education, such as:

- Books,
- Tuition;
- Testing fees,
- Lab fees, etc.

For an individual, these educational fees are claimed on Schedule A as a miscellaneous expense.

The Taxpayer Relief Act of 1997 added two new education tax credits to the code. Credits operate as a direct dollar-for-dollar reduction of your tax. The first is the so-called HOPE credit. The HOPE credit can give you a tax credit of up to $1,500 per year for the first two years of a post-secondary degree program. To qualify, you must be at least a part-time student. For the details, see IRS Publication 970, *Tax Benefits for Higher Education*.

The second credit is the lifetime learning credit. The lifetime learning credit is a credit of 20 percent of up to $5,000 of tuition and expenses for graduate and undergraduate courses. You must be enrolled on at least a half-time basis in a degree or certificate program. However, if you need the education to acquire or improve job skills, the half-time enrollment rule does not apply. You cannot claim both the HOPE credit and the lifetime learning credit. In addition, your credit is limited if you take a distribution from an education IRA. See Publication 970 for more details.

The Taxpayer Relief Act also added a provision allowing for the deduction of interest paid on student loans. In 1999, up to $1,500 of interest can be deducted and the amount grows to $2,500 for 2000 and after.

To qualify for the deduction, you must be at least a half-time student in post-secondary education or vocational training. The deduction may be claimed only for the first sixty months of interest on the debt. However, any period of time the loan is in deferral does not count against the time limit.

Job Hunting Fees

Code section 162 allows a person to deduct the costs incurred in seeking new employment. To be deductible, however, the search must be for a job within your current trade or business. The search does not have to be successful in order to claim the deduction. Nor does one have to be employed in order to claim the deduction. However, if unemployed while seeking the new job, the new job must be in the same trade or business as the previous job. Further, there can be no more than a few months unemployment between jobs for the expenses to be deductible.

Deductible job hunting expenses include:

- Air fare;
- Automobile and other transportation expenses;
- Employment agency fees;
- Costs of typing and printing résumés or similar items;
- Postage and other shipping costs;
- Long distance calls or faxes; and
- Advertising.

Travel expenses to another city are fully deductible even if you pursue personal activities while there. The rule is, if the trip is primarily related to hunting for a new job, you may deduct all expenses. A trip is considered primarily related to job hunting if you spend most of your time on the trip looking for work. To establish the purpose of the trip, keep a log of your activities to prove how much time you spent job hunting. See chapter nine for more on creating logs.

Even if the trip is not primarily related to finding work, you can nevertheless deduct specific expenses related to seeking employment. These include local transportation and other job hunting expenses incurred at the destination. IRS Publication 463, *Travel, Entertainment, Gift and Car Expenses*, has more information on this topic.

Investment Expenses

Under code section 212, all expenses incurred in the "production of income" are generally deductible. If the production of income expenses are not related to a full-time trade or business, the expenses are considered miscellaneous deductions taken on Schedule A. Of course, any expense related to the income of a business is not subject to the Schedule A limitation. It may be claimed on Schedule C.

Investors are a prime example of those who may claim expenses for the production of income. Such expenses include:

- Investment counseling fees;
- Subscription fees;
- Account custodian fees;
- State and local transfer fees;
- Fees for clerical help;
- Office rent; etc.

In fact, the law does not limit the deduction to just expenses incurred in the production of income. It goes much beyond that to include:

- Collection of income;
- Management of property;
- Maintenance of property; or
- Conservation of property held to produce income.

Thus, any expense that fairly falls into the categories listed above can be deducted. Those expenses expressly related to rents or royalty income are not subject to the limitation applicable to miscellaneous deductions. They are deducted from gross income using Schedule E. In IRS Publication 529, *Miscellaneous Deductions*, you find more information on this topic.

Legal Fees

Many people, including tax professionals, think of legal fees as non-deductible personal expenses. For the most part, this is true. But, there is an important exception. To the extent that legal fees are incurred in the production or collection of income or for the management, maintenance or conservation of property, they are deductible as a miscellaneous deduction.

When the legal fees are incurred as a result of the operation of a specific business, they are deductible as a business expense. Those of an individual are miscellaneous itemized deductions.

Unreimbursed Employee Business Expenses

This is a broad category of expenses you might incur as an employee. When these expenses are incurred for the purposes of earning income in connection with your job and they are not fully reimbursed by your employer, the unreimbursed portion is deductible. Most of these expenses are reported on Form 2106 and are deductible to the extent that they exceed 2 percent of adjusted gross income.

When considering whether an expense is deductible or not, keep in mind the general rule. When the expense is "ordinary and necessary" and is incurred for the "purposes of earning income," it is a deductible expense. The following are many of the deductible expenses that are often overlooked:

- Advertising costs;
- Answering service or machine when required by employer;
- Auto expense;
- Books or manuals used on the job;
- Briefcases used for business;
- Business cards or stationery if not supplied by employer;
- Business machines (computers are discussed later);
- Cleaning costs;
- Convention trips;
- Employment agency fees for getting the job;
- Entertainment expenses;
- Fidelity or performance bonds where required by the job;
- Furniture used for business;
- Gifts to customers;
- Home office expenses if you meet the rules *and* the home office is maintained for the convenience of the employer.
- Insurance premiums for work related coverage;
- Legal fees for work related issues;
- Lodging costs;
- Magazines and periodicals used for business;
- Meals out of town or with clients or customers;
- Medical examinations necessary for the job;
- Membership dues for trade or professional associations;
- Parking fees;

- Postage and other mailing or packaging costs;
- Rental costs for equipment, storage, etc.;
- Safety shoes or work boots;
- Spiffs for sales leads;
- Telephone expenses and long distance fees;
- Tolls;
- Travel expenses including airfare, cabs, etc.;
- Uniforms and other specialty clothing not usable off the job;
- Union dues and fees;

If you regularly incur expenses in any of these areas, it is advisable to create a separate recordkeeping log for each expense. The log should show the date, the nature of the expense, the business purpose and the amount of the expense. Keep your logs in thirty-day periods and have them notarized at the end of that period. They become sworn statements and are very powerful for proving the nature and amount of your unreimbursed business expenses. Be sure to use IRS Form 2106 to report unreimbursed business expenses on Schedule A. The next two chapters of this book show you exactly how to keep such logs and to use other recordkeeping tricks and secrets to increase deductions. Publication 529, *Miscellaneous Deductions*, provides more information on this topic.

Computers and Cellular Phones

For the self-employed, computers and cell phones are assets that can be depreciated. As explained in the previous chapter, code section 179 allows a citizen to make an election to deduct a capital asset (that is, "write it off") up to a stated amount each year. Thus, if you purchase a $3,000 computer, you can make the election on Form 4562 to take the full $3,000 as an expense in the year incurred, rather than depreciating the computer provided you meet the rules.

If you are an employee, computers and cell phones are deductible but you must meet two rules. First, the computer must be used for the convenience of your employer. Second, it must be a condition of your employment. To satisfy the first rule, you must be able to prove that your employer requires a computer for the job but does not provide one. To satisfy the second rule, the computer must be "inextricably related" to proper job performance.

Computers and cell phones--like autos--are considered "listed property" for depreciation and section 179 purposes. As previously explained in chapter seven, listed property is that which is susceptible to a high degree of personal use. It includes autos, photo equipment, TVs and similar items.

If the computer or other listed property is not used more than 50 percent in business, your depreciation deduction is limited and you cannot take the section 179 expense. Therefore, in order to expense your computer under section 179 and take the full deduction in the year purchased, you have to keep careful records to substantiate more than 50 percent business use.

In addition to meeting the two rules expressed above, the following elements must be proved to substantiate a section 179 deduction for a computer or cell phone:

- The cost of the listed property and other items such as repairs and maintenance;
- The dates of use;
- The name of the user;
- The business purpose of the item.

On the tax return claiming the deduction, be prepared to answer the following questions:

- The date the property was placed in service;
- The percentage of business use;
- Whether evidence is available to support the percentage of business use claimed; and
- Whether the evidence is written.

A log showing the use of your computer greatly helps carry the burden of proof. Revenue regulations expressly state that while a log is "not required," its value is much greater in proving the claim than other forms of evidence. Get into the habit of using logs to prove your entitlement to this and other deductions. For more on logs and how to create them, see chapter nine of this book. See IRS Publication 946, *How to Depreciate Property*, for more details.

Commuting Expenses

The costs you incur in getting yourself to work each day are considered commuting costs. They are generally non-deductible personal expenses. Even if you live a long distance from work, cannot find suitable living accommodations close to work or cannot find work close to home, the expense is non-deductible.

There are a couple of exceptions to this rule, however. One or more may apply to you. If they do, you will see a substantial increase in your deduction for auto expenses. One exception applies when additional costs are incurred for the transportation of tools or equipment to work. When your costs of transportation increase because of the need to transport tools or equipment, you are entitled to deduct the costs over and above your normal commuting expenses. The IRS gives this example in Revenue Ruling 75-380, 1975-2 CB 59:

> Example: A taxpayer commuted to and from work by public transportation before the taxpayer was required to carry necessary work implements. It cost $2 per day to commute to and from work. When it became necessary to carry the implements to and from work, it cost $3 per day to drive a car and an additional $5 per day to rent a trailer in which the implements were carried. The allowable deduction is the $5 per day additional expense that the taxpayer incurred in renting the trailer to carry the work implements.

Transportation from one job site to another is not considered commuting. When you travel from home to the first job site, you incur non-deductible commuting expenses. But when you go from the first job site to another, that travel is considered deductible. The purpose of the travel from one site to another must be primarily for business. Further, if you extend your trip for some non-business reason, such as to stop at the grocery store along the way, the additional mileage is not deductible.

The deduction for such travel is allowed even when it happens to correspond with your normal commute. A good example is found in the case of *Lopkoff vs. Commissioner*, TC Memo 1982-701, 45 TCM 256 (Tax Court, 1982). Lopkoff worked at a hospital thirty miles from her home. She had a second job of picking up and delivering x-rays between the hospital she worked at and one near her home. Despite the IRS' objection, the Tax Court allowed her a deduction for the costs of traveling between the two hospitals because the costs were ordinary and necessary expenses connected with her delivery business.

Another exception to the general rule is when the job is temporary. When you are stationed at a temporary assignment away from your normal work place, the costs of commuting are deductible. This is true even if you go home after each workday. To benefit, the job must be temporary, as opposed to either "indefinite" or "indeterminate." The job is considered temporary if it is expected to end in a relatively short time and that fact is foreseeable. If you do not know how long a job will last, the job is indefinite or indeterminate.

If you maintain an office in your home that is your "principal place of business" as defined in the previous chapter, all of your travel to outside work sites is deductible business mileage. This is true whether it is overnight travel to a distant city or whether it is across town to see a client or customer. Whenever you claim a deduction for commuting mileage, be sure you have a log to prove the date of the travel, miles, and business purpose of the travel. Publication 463, *Travel, Entertainment, Gift and Car Expenses*, has more information on this topic.

Moving Expenses

Changes in the tax laws reduced the amount of moving expenses a person can claim. However, contrary to what many believe, they have not been eliminated. With some limitations, code section 217 provides two categories of deductible moving expenses. They are:

- Expenses for moving your household furnishings and personal items to your new residence; and
- Expenses for your transportation, including lodging, you incur traveling to your new home.

To be deductible, the expenses must be reasonable. Lavish expenses are not allowed, nor are expenses that do not reflect the shortest, most direct route. In addition, the expenses are deductible only if you move for purposes of commencing work. It can be your first job, a new job or continuation of an existing job in a new location.

To claim the deduction, you must meet the mileage test. The distance from your former home to your new place of work must be at least 50 miles *farther* than the distance from your previous home to your previous place of work. If you had no previous place of work, the new job must be at least 50 miles from your former home. In measuring the distance, you must use the shortest, most direct routes.

These expenses are considered deductible costs associated with moving personal items and household goods:

- Direct shipping fees paid to movers;
- Operating costs of your own vehicle used to move your items;
- Costs of shipping an auto;
- Costs of moving a pet;
- Fees, taxes and other costs imposed on moving your items;
- Fees for in-transit storage of your items;
- Insurance costs for your items, whether incurred in connection with the move or in-transit storage;
- Pre-move expenses such as packing and crating costs;
- Costs of disconnecting utilities in order to move appliances or similar items;
- Post-move expenses such as costs for unpacking and preparation for use of your items; and
- Costs to re-connect appliances that have been moved (not including phone).

These expenses are considered deductible expenses associated with transporting yourself and your family to the new residence:

- Gasoline and oil;
- Auto repairs or maintenance incurred along the way;
- As an alternative to actual auto expenses, you may claim a standard mileage allowance of nine cents per mile;
- Tolls and parking fees;
- Lodging costs, but not meals. Deductible lodging is limited to the day you arrive at the new residence and one day after your old residence becomes unusable; and
- Other transportation fees, including airfare or cabs.

The deduction for transportation costs are limited to just one trip but family members do not have to travel together. If you are self-employed and are moving your business equipment or furniture, these expenses are deductible on your Schedule C as ordinary business expenses. Otherwise, they are miscellaneous itemized deductions taken on Schedule A subject to the two percent limitation. Use IRS Form 3903 to report moving expenses. Other limitations apply and there are special rules applicable to foreign moves. For more information, see IRS Publication 521, *Moving Expenses*.

Casualty Loss

Code section 165 allows a deduction for casualty or theft losses. The loss is measured by the actual damage to the property in question. The damage must be caused by a sudden, unpredictable or unusual event. Either human or natural forces can cause it. Such events can include:

- Fire;
- Theft;
- Flood;
- Tornado;
- Hurricane;
- Airplane crash;
- Embezzlement;

- Earthquake;
- Earthslide;
- Burst water heater;
- Vandalism;
- Bank failure;
- Cave in;
- Sonic boom;
- Bomb damage;
- Lightning;
- Broken water lines;
- Power failure;
- Damage due to unusually heavy rain;
- Quarry blast;
- Insect damage;
- Chemical damage to lawn or landscaping;
- Machine damage to septic system or drain field;
- Frost or freeze damage;
- Jewelry lost in sink drain;
- Drought when sudden and severe;
- Car crash;
- Riot damage;
- Shipwreck;
- Smog damage;
- Snow; and
- Volcanic eruption.

There are three limitations that apply to this deduction. First, you cannot deduct the first $100 of any casualty loss. Second, casualty losses are deductible only to the extent that they exceed casualty gains. A casualty gain may arise if you are reimbursed by your insurance company for more than your basis in the property damaged. Third, total casualty losses are deductible only to the extent they exceed 10 percent of your adjusted gross income. This deduction is not subject to the itemized deduction phase out rule for high-income citizens.

Use IRS Form 4684 to claim casualty and theft loss deductions on your tax return. Please see IRS Publication 584, *Casualty, Disaster and Theft Loss Workbook* for more information.

Charitable Contributions

All of us realize that cash contributions made to charitable organizations are deductible. But did you know you can also claim a charitable contribution for the costs you incur in spending your own time and money on charitable causes? You cannot deduct the value of any services given to, or time spent on the charitable project, but you can deduct the out-of-pocket costs associated with it.

Revenue Regulation section 1.170A-1(g) provides as follows:

> Contributions of services. No deduction is allowable under section 170 for a contribution of services. However, unreimbursed expenditures made incident to the rendition of services to an organization contributions to which are deductible may constitute a deductible contribution. For example, the cost of a uniform without general utility which is required to be worn in performing donated services is deductible. Similarly, out-of-pocket transportation expenses necessarily incurred in performing donated services are deductible. Reasonable expenditures for meals and lodging necessarily incurred while away from home in the course of performing donated services also are deductible.

The expenses must be reasonable to be deductible. When away from home, expenses are deductible only if there is no significant element of personal pleasure, recreation or vacation in the travel. To show the fact that these elements were not a significant portion of the travel, keep a log showing the activities you engaged in while traveling for charitable purposes. The following out-of-pocket items can be claimed:

- Gasoline and oil;
- Auto repairs or maintenance incurred along the way;
- As an alternative to actual auto expenses, you may claim a standard charitable mileage allowance of 14 cents per mile;
- Tolls and parking fees;

- Lodging costs;
- Meals;
- Other transportation fees, including airfare or cabs.

Expenses for meals and lodging are deductible only if you are away from home performing charitable service. Transportation expenses are deductible whether you are away from home or not.

The deduction is not limited to travel expenses. In fact, any out-of-pocket, unreimbursed expense you incur for the purpose of rendering services to qualified charitable organizations is deductible. These include:

- Telephone or long distance charges;
- Uniforms needed for charitable work;
- Expenses of operating and maintaining equipment or machinery directly attributable to using the equipment to perform gratuitous services for a charitable organization. The cost of the equipment itself is not deductible unless donated to the charity;
- Expenses to repair or refurbish property used exclusively by a charitable organization;
- Office or similar supplies used in connection with charitable service; and
- Advertising fees and costs related to charitable activity.

To be assured of the deduction, you must meet the following rules:

- The expense must be incurred directly in connection with and be solely attributable to charitable services;
- A substantial, direct, personal benefit cannot be derived by anyone other than the charitable organization;
- You must actually provide the service to the charity in question; and
- The services must further the activities of the charitable organization.

I recommend you review the section in the next chapter dealing with recordkeeping for charitable contributions. Follow the rules for proving charitable contributions. This ensures you have adequate proof of your out-of-pocket expenses incurred in connection with providing gratis services to a church or charity. See IRS Publication 526, *Charitable Contributions*, for more information.

Pre-Paid Interest--"Points"--on Home Mortgage

Points charged by mortgage lenders in connection with your home loan are generally considered pre-paid interest. One point generally is equal to one percent of the mortgage amount. As we learned in chapter seven, the general rule is that no deduction is allowed for pre-paid interest. Generally speaking, pre-payments of interest must be capitalized then deducted in the year to which the interest applies. This rule, however, does not apply to points charged for a home mortgage.

Code section 461(g)(2) provides that points are deductible in the year paid if:

- The debt is incurred for the purposes of acquiring or improving your principal residence;
- The payment of points is an established practice in your area; and,
- The number of points charged does not exceed that generally charged in your area.

To be deductible, you cannot use the money borrowed to pay off existing indebtedness, even if the loan is a refinance arrangement. Under those circumstances, the points must be amortized over the term of the loan. However, if a portion of the loan proceeds pays off prior debt and a portion is used to improve the home, you may pro rate the points and deduct the portion attributable to the home improvements.

Sometimes there is a question whether charges made by your lender are actually points or whether they constitute something else. A point is deductible when it constitutes interest, which is defined by law as a charge for the use of money. Regardless of what other title the lender may ascribe to the payment, if it is a charge for the use of money and not for services provided by the lender, it is deductible as pre-paid interest. Other names might include:

- Loan origination fee (if denominated as one percent of the loan);
- Loan discount fee;
- Loan discount points;
- Discount points;
- Processing fees; or
- Premium fees.

In 1994, the IRS issued a Revenue Procedure to give guidance on the issue. If you meet the so-called "safe harbor" set forth in Rev. Proc. 94-27, 1994-15 IRB 17, your payment is treated as pre-paid interest and is deductible in the year paid. You must meet the three requirements set forth above, in addition to the following three items:

- The amount must be clearly designated on the settlement statement as "loan origination fees," "discount points," etc.;
- The amount must be computed as a percentage of the loan; and
- The amount must be paid directly by the borrower from separate funds, not funds borrowed as a part of the principal transaction.

To meet the last rule, plan to do one of two things. First, make a sufficient down payment so as to accommodate payment of the added points. As long as your down payment is sufficient to cover all such items, you are considered to have paid the items separately. As an alternative, make a separate check payable to the lender in satisfaction of all points. Pay the points at closing and designate on the face of the check the fact that the payment is for points charged in connection with the loan.

It is actually possible for you, as the purchaser of a home, to claim a deduction for points paid by the seller. Often, the seller offers to pay a point or two in order to make his home more attractive on the market. When the seller pays the points, the money is considered to have come from a source other than borrowed money. As a result, they are deductible by the purchaser. However, to get the benefit, the purchaser must reduce the basis in the property by an amount equal to the deduction.

Points paid on refinance loans, if not used all or in part to improve your principal residence, are deducted ratably over the period of the loan. If you refinance your home over fifteen years and pay $2,000 in points, your annual deduction in addition to mortgage interest is $13. IRS Publication 530, *Tax Information for First-time Homeowners*, provides more details on this and other interest-related issues.

Tax Credits for Children

There are three credits under the law applicable to raising children. Because they are credits, the amount of the credit operates as a dollar-for-dollar reduction of your tax liability. Let us examine the three credits that can cut your tax if you are a parent.

The Child and Dependent Care Credit. Under code section 21, a credit is allowed for a portion of the childcare expenses incurred for working families. There are seven criteria you must meet in order to claim the credit. They are:

- You must have one or more children living in your home;
- The childcare expenses must be incurred to allow you to work or look for work;
- You must have income from work during the year the credit is claimed;
- The payment for childcare must be made to someone you or your spouse could not claim as a dependent. If the payments were made to your own child, that child must be nineteen or over by the end of the year;
- You must file a joint return if married;
- You must use Form 1040 or Form 1040A. You cannot use Form 1040 EZ;

- You must provide the IRS with specified information on persons who performed the childcare services. See code section 21 and IRS Publication 503, *Child and Dependent Care Expenses*.

You may be entitled to claim a childcare credit even if the person you are taking care of is not a child. The law allows a credit for "dependents" who are not children, if the person is physically or mentally incapable of taking care of himself. Code section 21(b)(1)(B). This applies even if you cannot claim the person as a dependent exemption on your own tax return.

The childcare credit is limited. First, the credit is only available for children under the age of thirteen. Secondly, there is a cap on the expenses that can be considered for purposes of figuring the credit. If there is just one person in the household for whom you are caring, the expense limitation is $2,400. If there are two or more persons in the household, the expense limitation is $4,800.

This does not mean you are entitled to a credit of those amounts. The credit is actually a percentage of those amounts, depending upon your adjusted gross income. However, in no event can you begin the calculation using more than $4,800 in costs for purposes of determining the credit. See code section 21(c). The actual credit is determined by applying your childcare costs (capped at either $2,400 or $4,800) against a percentage. The percentage varies depending upon your adjusted gross income. The highest possible percentage, applying to those with adjusted gross income up to $10,000, is 30 percent. The lowest percentage, applying to those with adjusted gross income of $28,000 or more, is 20 percent. Code section 21(a)(1) and (2).

Accordingly, the largest possible credit a person could receive is $1,440. To receive that amount requires that you earn $10,000 or less, have at least two children and pay at least $4,800 per year in childcare expenses. As your income rises, the percentage available drops. Those making $28,000 per year or more have a maximum potential credit of $960 (4,800 x .2). See IRS Publication 503, for a chart on the different percentages for the credit.

The Child Tax Credit. The general child tax credit is a credit of $500 per child you claim as a dependent on your tax return. The credit is available for each child under age seventeen. The credit is phased out for citizens with adjusted gross income in excess of $75,000 for single filers and $110,000 for joint filers.

The Adoption Credit. The third credit is the adoption credit. It allows a tax credit of up to $5,000 per child or $6,000 for a child with special needs, for the costs of adoption. The costs include adoption fees, court costs, attorney's fees and other expenses that are connected with the adoption. The credit is not available if the costs of adoption are claimed as a deduction. For more on this credit, See IRS Publication 968, *Tax Benefits for Adoption.*

Conclusion

Please note that the discussion throughout this book is based upon the current state of the law. We all know that the tax code is an evolutionary beast, constantly subject to change. You do yourself a disservice if you do not verify that the statements of law contained in this book are binding for any year in which you may wish to apply the material. For that reason, the *Pilla Talks Taxes* monthly newsletter is extremely beneficial in keeping readers up to date with current, relevant tax law changes.

CHAPTER NINE
How To Keep Good Records

In more than two decades of experience dealing with the IRS I find that most people pay too much in taxes. This happens because people either 1) do not understand their rights when it comes to deductions, credits, etc., or 2) are concerned that if they claim all they are entitled to, they will draw the IRS' attention to themselves--something nobody wants to do. So concerned are people about maintaining a low profile when it comes to the IRS that most willingly leave deductions on the table. It has even come to the point where many tax professionals actually advise people not to claim their legal deductions for fear of raising the red flag.

The reality, however, is that not claiming all the deductions you are entitled to does not afford any audit protection. All it does is guarantee that you will pay more taxes. The key to controlling your tax liability and providing audit protection at the same time is to be sure you can prove that all the entries in your return are accurate. In fact, the vast majority of disputes with the IRS involve claims by the agency that citizens have inadequate records to support their deductions. The solution to the problem, therefore, is to claim all the deductions you are entitled to claim but to have the documents necessary to back them up.

In my book, *IRS, Taxes and the Beast*, I document the fact that the IRS often uses bluff and intimidation in the audit process to get people to pay taxes they do not owe. I prove in that book how the IRS convinces people that their return is inaccurate by challenging the adequacy of their records. The reality is, the IRS is wrong in its audit results as much as 60 to 90 percent of the time. To overcome this problem, you must understand what good records are and how to keep them. That is the topic of this chapter.

What Good Records Accomplish

Adequate records optimize your ability to claim deductions, allowances, credits and exemptions which in turn reduces your tax bite. As such, you are directly compensated for the time it takes to keep adequate records by a reduction in your tax burden.

Furthermore, the law places an affirmative obligation upon each citizen to keep records necessary to determine his correct tax liability. Code section 6001. Stated another way, you bear the burden to prove that the claims in your return are correct. Do not be misled by the media claims that the burden of proof was shifted to the IRS by the IRS Restructuring and Reform Act. The fact is, that shift is very limited and will impact fewer than 3 percent of the cases. It remains true that, absent adequate records, the IRS is at liberty to--and regularly does--add additional income to your tax return and disallows deductions. Code section 446(b). Please see *IRS, Taxes and the Beast* for a complete discussion on how to defend a tax audit in all situations.

What are "Adequate" Records?

In more than seventeen *thousand* pages of law and regulation, one would think it unlikely that the tax code is at all deficient. Nevertheless it is. The tax code *does not* define what constitutes adequate records in any but a precious few circumstances. No general rules, guidelines or standards exist to guide one in ascertaining whether his year-long recordkeeping sojourn is worth the scraps of paper it is written on. Tax auditors know this and they deliberately take advantage of it.

Consequently, those unaware of what constitutes adequate records almost always end up owing more taxes if challenged by the IRS. But the hassle is avoided entirely when you understand precisely what "good records" are. Follow closely as we examine my complete recordkeeping system. This system allows you to keep proper records of all income and deductions. Using it can lead to a reduction in the taxes you pay.

Recording Your Income

The power of the IRS to wreak havoc on your financial life is not limited to the ability to disallow deductions. An even more potent weapon is the agency's ability to "determine" your income based upon "available information" or by using statistical data. One entire audit program uses these very techniques. The program is known as the economic reality audit and is designed to ascertain hidden income by examining every element of your lifestyle including your home, furniture, fixtures, clothing, jewelry, etc. I discuss this program at length in *IRS, Taxes and the Beast*.

In the absence of adequate records of income or in the event you fail to file a return, the IRS is permitted to determine your income for you. It may do so using the total of all deposits to your bank account. It may compute changes in your net worth or use statistical data compiled either by the agency itself or other agencies of government. The most favored source of statistical data is Bureau of Labor statistics. These data set forth average incomes earned by individuals within a particular element of the work force and within a given geographical location.

In *IRS, Taxes and the Beast*, I explain how the IRS uses four different audit methods to increase your reported income. I refer to this practice as adding *phantom income* to a tax return. Phantom income is income that exists only on IRS' accounting ledgers--not in your pocket. There are two specific techniques for avoiding a phantom income determination. Let us address them here.

Bank Records. Bank account information is perhaps the number one tool used to add phantom income to a return. For example, suppose a dishonest citizen claims he earned $20,000 during a given year but deposited $30,000 to his bank account. The IRS quickly draws the conclusion that $10,000 is unreported income.

Conversely, bank account records operate well to the honest citizen's advantage. The bank itself makes an indisputable record of each deposit you make to your account. When all your income is deposited, the bank's own records show the total of those deposits. Should the IRS allege that you failed to report a portion of your income, bank records allow you to counter that claim with firm evidence. Provided you can testify that all your income was in fact deposited to the account, the IRS cannot sustain a claim of unreported income.

Carefully document bank deposits that do not constitute taxable income. Examples include gifts or loan proceeds. Bank records do not explain the source and nature of the deposits. The records merely show the deposit of checks or cash and the amount. If total bank deposits exceed your declared income, be prepared to demonstrate that the source of the deposit is a non-taxable source of income. If you cannot, the IRS considers the deposit to be taxable income.

Ledgers or Log Books. Ledgers or log books are contemporaneous records of income (or expenses). Without a doubt, they are the best weapons against any assault on the veracity of your tax return. Contemporaneous ledgers or logs are made at the time of the occurrence of the events being recorded. When done properly, they are unassailable and provide the basis for audit-proofing the income claimed in your return. We discuss audit-proofing in detail in the next chapter.

How to Make Foolproof Records of Income

Independently log all your income. Do not rely on third parties to make your records. By making your own records, you eliminate the potential that third party errors will haunt you. Let me give you an example. Tim worked for a local radio station. He received a Form W-2 as an employee of the station. In addition, he did independent production work for other companies. Those companies issued a Form 1099 to report payments to Tim. However, one company failed to submit the form on time. Because Tim relied solely on third party records as his only recordkeeping system, he did not report the income on his tax return.

Approximately eighteen months after filing, the company discovered the oversight, then issued the 1099. The IRS received the form and as they do with all information returns, cross-checked it with Tim's tax return. Tim under-reported his income by the amount shown on the 1099. He did not intend to deceive the IRS. He merely failed to keep his own records of income.

The IRS corrected Tim's return based upon the Form 1099. Shortly thereafter, the IRS levied Tim's paycheck for the additional tax, interest and penalty. The entire ordeal could have been avoided if Tim made and kept his own records of the income he earned during the year.

To record your income, create a log for each source of income you receive during the year. Each log should show the date of the income, the nature of the payment, the payor and the amount of withholding for state and federal taxes, if any. The following examples illustrate specific income logs.

Wages and Salaries. Make an entry in your wages log each time you receive a paycheck. Transfer all data shown on the check stub to the wages log. If you receive tip income during the year, create a separate log for tip income. Your tip income log should have an entry for each day you work, rather than for each payday. The reason is tips are earned on a daily basis and therefore should be recorded as such. If tips are paid by the employer periodically with wages, include the tips on the wages log under a separate heading.

Rents and Royalties. Create a separate log for rents or royalties income. Make the entries as you receive the payments. Be sure to indicate the source of the income, such as from a particular asset or property. Generally, rent and royalty payments are not subject to withholding. However, certain royalty payments may be subjected to backup withholding if your social security number is not verified to the payor. If this is the case, indicate the amount of any withholding from the payment in the appropriate column. Also, your estimated tax payments should be noted in an appropriate column.

Interest and Dividends. Make all entries in this log as payments are received. In the payor column, note whether you were paid interest on a bond or checking account, etc., or dividends on stocks or mutual funds, etc. Indicate the specific source of the payment. In an appropriate column, indicate whether any backup withholding was taken. Lastly, note whether the payment is taxable or not. Certain interest payments on federal, state and local bonds are not taxable. Determine whether your payments are subject to taxation and note that accordingly.

Stock Transactions. A stock transactions log is a means of simplifying the data transmitted in your monthly brokerage statement. These statements can be difficult to read. My format allows a convenient way of tracking all stock purchases and sales. This enables you to quickly determine the gain or loss incurred in connection with any stock transaction. From left to right, the entries should be: buy date; sell date; name of stock; number of shares; price each; total purchase price; gain or loss.

Because you purchase and sell a specific block of stock just once, you can record all stock transactions in a continuing format, running the log from year to year. The gain or loss on a stock is computed and entered after you sell.

Pensions and Annuities. In the payor column, indicate the company making the payment and the type of plan under which it is made. Also note the amount of the payment and record any withholding.

Estates and Trusts. In the payor column, indicate the source of the payment. Make a note as to the purpose of the payment, whether, for example it was an inheritance or trust distribution. This enables you to later determine whether that particular payment constitutes taxable income. Be sure to note any backup withholding or estimated tax payments withheld from the payment.

Self-employed, Partnerships and S Corporations. If you derive income from self-employment, partnerships or through an S corporation (other than wages or dividends), maintain a log reflecting such payments. Express the payments in terms of gross amounts. This is because any deductions, such as for costs of goods or operating expenses, are shown in a corresponding expense ledger. We examine expense logs later.

In the case of self-employment income, there is a firm duty to make estimated payments against your tax liability. Record the quarterly payments as you make them. Also, if you earn income from a variety of sources or customers, you may wish to create a log for each source or customer. In that manner, you can track receipts more specifically.

In the book, *IRS, Taxes and the Beast*, I present a number of case studies on how citizens used income logs to defeat IRS claims of unreported income. That book takes you step-by-step through the process of defending such a claim. However, you should note that defeating a claim of unreported income is difficult if you have improper or incomplete income records. Using the income log format outlined above puts you in the strongest possible position to defeat the IRS' claim.

Recording Your Deductions

Each tax return contains two elements. The citizen signing the return must prove both. The first element is that of *income*. We addressed that issue above. The second element is a bit trickier. It is the element of *deductions*. You bear the burden to prove that each deduction claimed is both legally permissible and was paid in the year claimed.

Earlier I mentioned that many citizens facing an audit have problems because they do not keep adequate records of their deductions. Often, those who have good records are bluffed into believing their records are not adequate. The result in either case is citizens pay more taxes than they owe. By understanding what constitutes adequate proof of deductions and keeping accurate records in the first place, you virtually eliminate the threat of having deductions disallowed.

How to Make Foolproof Records of Deductions

There are six legally acceptable ways to prove deductions. Four of the six methods involve contemporaneous records. These are records made at the time of the occurrence of the event being recorded. Contemporaneous records are the soundest method of proving deductions. The following discussion addresses each of the six methods.

Cash Receipts. Cash receipts must contain a date, a description of the items purchased, the amount of the purchase and the name of the vendor from whom purchased. You may add comments to allow a potential auditor to see at a glance how the item relates to a deductible expenditure. For example, if you purchase bolts from a hardware store for use in your business, make a note indicating the business use to which they are put.

Canceled Checks. Canceled checks must contain precisely the same information as shown above. Use the "memo" portion of the check to record descriptive information and make further notes if necessary in your check register. Do not fail to complete the check blank and register as fully as possible. It could help you later.

Year-end Statements. Year-end statements are summaries of expenditures made by third parties. Examples of year-end statements are those 1) issued by mortgage companies indicating the amount of interest paid during the year, 2) statements by churches showing your contributions, and 3) statements by county tax assessors reflecting the real estate taxes paid. These statements are perhaps the best method of proving a deduction because they come from third parties and contain all the necessary information in a single document.

Take time to seek third party statements from as many persons or businesses as possible. For example, a letter to a supplier seeking a statement reflecting purchases during the year will surely result in a year-end statement. This greatly aids your ability to prepare and file an accurate and audit-proofed return.

Log Books. Log books are utilized to prove deductions as well as verify income. Any expense you incur on a regular basis should be recorded in a log. This is particularly true if the expense is paid in cash. The log book, coupled with cash receipts, nails down your burden of proof with respect to that deduction. Examples of expenses where log books should be used regardless of how the expense is paid are mileage, lodging, meals and entertainment. Using log books puts you ahead of the average citizen when it comes to defending your deductions.

Reconstructions. Reconstructions are used when there are no supporting documents for a deduction. It is perhaps the least known method of proving deductions. The reason is the IRS has convinced us that without a piece of paper to support the expense, the expense is simply not allowed. This is not true. When done correctly, reconstructions are every bit as valid as the other methods of proof.

Here is an example. Kathy was a traveling sales representative for a clothing firm. For three years, she traveled across five states. As an independent contractor, she was responsible to pay all of her own expenses, including travel. These expenses climbed into the tens of thousands of dollars for each year she was on the road. For some reason, her personal records were lost. When called in for an audit of her tax returns, she did not have one scrap of paper to document a trip around the block.

To defend her return, she undertook the process of reconstructing three years of her life. The starting point was her address book where she recorded the names and addresses of the retailers who purchased her wares. Because she used her American Express card quite often while on the road, she mailed a letter to American Express requesting copies of the monthly bills. Charge card slips are itemized with a name, address, date and description of the item charged. As such, most of Kathy's hotel and meal charges could be shown through the slips. When she received the American Express material, Kathy undertook the process of retracing her steps.

The first charge slip showed she spent a night in Fargo, North Dakota. Looking then to her list of actual and prospective customers, she determined and listed on a separate sheet each of the retailers she called upon in Fargo and the immediate area. When she was able to pin down the specific amounts spent on food and fuel, they were noted. When she was unable to do so, she estimated the amounts based upon reason and common sense. She followed this process for each of the thirty-six months at issue. It enabled her to document nearly all of the expenses incurred during the periods in question. Eventually the IRS allowed the reconstructions--to the penny!

Be Aware: By their nature, reconstructions are estimates. To the best extent possible, they attempt to re-create a picture of reality as it was in years past. Because they are not self-contained as are canceled checks or cash receipts, they must be supported with oral testimony. More on this later.

For example, in many cases, Kathy's charge slips showed a hotel expense. This proved she spent the night in a hotel but did not show any cost of food. Common sense dictates one must eat on a daily basis. For that reason, she carefully provided testimony to the effect that food was purchased on those days when no food charges were shown by the credit card receipts. When used in conjunction with oral testimony, reconstructions are an effective method of proving deductions.

Testimony. Testimony is nothing more than oral declarations by the citizen to the effect that the amounts claimed were in fact paid. When such proof is offered to an auditor, the most common response is something such as, "Well, I am sure you are telling the truth but I cannot take your word for it. I must have some kind of proof." This statement assumes your word is not "proof." However, courts regularly allow deductions when the only proof offered by the citizen is testimony, i.e., his word. How is that so?

Provided the testimony is plausible, believable and credible, the court cannot refuse to consider it. Testimony meeting these criteria is just as valid as any piece of paper you can name. Let me prove it.

Tom was a regular churchgoer. Every Sunday, he and his family attended weekly services at the local church. Every Sunday, Tom deposited money in the collection basket. He gave cash, usually $40, each Sunday. At the end of the year, Tom deducted $1,980 from his income tax return as a charitable contribution.

He was later audited. The auditor requested proof of the $1,980 contribution. Tom did not have any substantiation because he gave cash. But he did explain to the agent what his practices were, why he engaged in the practices and that without a doubt, he did give the money. The auditor was not impressed. After resolution of all other issues, Tom took an appeal on the question of his deductions. His case ended up before the Tax Court.

During the trial, Tom testified as to his practices and the reasons for them. The judge kindly asked Tom questions about his habits and how he was able to determine the amount he gave. Tom's answers were direct and to the point. They were sensible and believable. All in all, Tom was honest and forthright with the judge during the trial.

In addition to his own testimony, Tom presented the testimony of the church pastor who corroborated the fact Tom was at church each Sunday. The pastor backed Tom's position that he always tithed with cash rather than by check. The pastor's attitude and demeanor was equally forthright.

The court ruled in Tom's favor. Specifically, the court held that his testimony and that of the pastor supported the deduction. As a result of this and other successes like it, your case will not likely go to court. When presented properly, the auditor will likely be forced to accept your deductions.

A word of caution: To be effective, oral testimony must be *specific.* Qualified claims and vague recollections will not carry the day. Be sure your explanations are seasoned with as many hard facts as humanly possible. Specificity leads to believability.

Oral testimony must be presented in the form of an affidavit. An affidavit is a sworn statement explaining the facts and circumstances of your claim. Your affidavit must explain exactly how your reconstructions were prepared. It must clearly and plainly describe the expenses shown in your reconstruction worksheets. Lastly, it must declare that you in fact paid the expenses in the year claimed. In the absence of contemporaneous records to back up your expenses, reconstructions and affidavits provide all the proof needed to settle the audit dispute favorably. My book *41 Ways to Lick the IRS with a Postage Stamp* provides detailed examples of affidavits and offers guidance on how to draft them.

How to Make Foolproof Records of Deductions

All the hassles growing from inadequate records, including the need to create affidavits, are avoided when you make contemporaneous logs of your expenses. Begin immediately to record your expenses in an organized fashion. Much of the April paper war is avoided if you organize yourself at the beginning of the year and carry that organization with you throughout the year. When faced with the April deadline, the lion's share of the work is done.

The log formats we are about to review are not designed to replace any accounting system installed by a competent accountant. However, they can augment any system, allowing you to keep careful track of where you spend your money. In each case, the log calls for an entry of a check number if the expense was paid by check. Enter the number to later recover that check quickly. When paying expenses in cash, keep the receipt. If for some reason the receipt is unavailable, be careful to verify the logs. We discuss this in more detail later. Following this procedure ensures the strength and stability of your logs.

Let us examine log formats that enable you to install an effective recordkeeping system to optimize deductions in every area.

Rents and Royalties. Persons deriving income from a rental business or royalties naturally incur expenses associated with operating that business. At a minimum, I suggest the following columns: date; payee; check number; taxes; repairs; insurance; utilities; legal and professional fees; interest. Also record any expense directly related to earning rent or royalty income. You may wish to add a miscellaneous column to record expenses that do not fall directly into one of the above categories.

Please note that mileage incurred with rental or royalty income is deductible. If you incur mileage in connection with the operation of more than one business, create a separate mileage log for each business.

Interest and Dividends. Expenses associated with earning interest and dividends is recorded in a log virtually identical to the one outlined above. You may wish to drop a particular column, such as repairs and add a column, such as commissions.

Estates and Trusts. It is not likely you have expenses directly related to earning income from an estate or trust. In most cases, the estate or trust has an administrator or trustee whose job is to conduct the business of the trust. If for some reason you do incur expenses on a regular basis relative to an estate or trust, create a log to record them. Use the categories set forth above. Certain adaptations may be in order based upon your circumstances.

Self-employed, Partnerships and S Corporations. A log of expenses related to the operation of a business must contain many more columns than those shown above. The reason is businesses incur a much wider range of expenses. Among the entries such a log must contain are: date; payee; check number; advertising; bad debts; car and truck expense; commissions and fees; depletion; depreciation; employee benefit programs; insurance; interest; legal and professional fees; office expenses; pension and profit sharing programs; rent or lease payments including lease of business equipment; repairs and maintenance; supplies; taxes and licenses; utilities; wages; postage; miscellaneous. Maintain a separate log for business travel, meals and entertainment. Use the mileage and travel logs discussed later.

Cost of Goods Sold. It is not uncommon for small business operators to fail to keep track of their business inventory purchases properly. Your business deduction for cost of goods sold will not be allowed unless you properly document purchases of inventory made during the course of the year. The IRS has a formula for arriving at the cost of goods deduction shown on the Schedule C. An integral part of the formula is total purchases made during the year. See IRS Schedule C, Part III (not shown here).

Those who benefit from a cost of goods log are those involved in direct sales of any kind. It is common for such persons to maintain a small inventory of products. Preparing a log optimizes the cost of goods deduction. The purpose of this log is to record in one place all inventory purchases needed to compute the Schedule C cost of goods expense. Your cost of goods log should contain columns for the date; check number; payee; description of the goods; amount.

Residential Improvements Log. Profit from the sale of a residence may or may not be taxable. In all events, you are taxed only on the profit. To compute the profit, you are allowed to take into consideration all the capital improvements made while you owned it.

For example, if you purchase a house for $50,000 make $20,000 worth of capital improvements (i.e., new siding, new furnace, new roof) then sell it for $70,000, you realize no gain on the sale. Hence, you are not taxed on the proceeds.

Most of us would have a record of a $2,000 roofing job or a $4,000 kitchen project because they were probably paid by check. The question is whether we would *remember* the expense when it comes time to compute the gain or loss from the sale. More importantly, most of us *do not* keep track of the more subtle improvements. Though they may be of a lesser amount, they are nevertheless deductible at the time of sale. For example, $50 worth of boards and $10 in nails to repair a deck are capital expenditures. Whenever you make a trip to the home improvement center or hardware store, be sure to make an entry in your residential improvements log. You will be surprised how fast the deductible expenses mount.

Data in the residential improvements log should include the date; check number; type of improvement; payee; amount.

Travel, Meals and Entertainment. List all travel, meals and entertainment expenses on a separate log. I recommend you segregate these expenses by business or activity. For example, if you incur expenses as an employee of a company and at the same time have your own small business, maintain two travel logs. This enables you to more easily organize your figures at the end of the year. Claim employee expenses on Form 2106 and travel related to your own business on Schedule C.

Data in such a log must include the date; purpose of travel and cities visited; amounts for fares, meals and lodging; entertainment expenditures. As to entertainment expenditures, you must include the name of the persons entertained; their relationship to your business; the business purpose of the entertainment; and the bona fide business discussions you had before, during or after the entertainment activity. Without such supplemental information, no record is adequate to prove entertainment expenses.

Mileage. Mileage expenses can be deducted under one of two methods. You may either deduct actual expenses for auto depreciation, fuel, oil, maintenance, etc., or you can claim the IRS' standard mileage allowance. Careful records, including odometer readings, are needed to support actual expenses. However, just a simple mileage log is needed to support the standard allowance claim. In either event, maintain a thorough log.

If you intend to deduct your actual expenses, including auto depreciation, record the total miles driven during the year. Keeping odometer readings accomplishes this. Your mileage log should include start-mileage and stop-mileage columns for this purpose. In a business miles column, note the portion of total miles driven that were business miles. These figures allow you to determine the percentage of driving that is business versus that which is personal. If the percentage is 65 percent business, you are entitled to deduct 65 percent for all actual auto expenses.

When utilizing the standard mileage allowance, one need not record expenses associated with operating the vehicle. To earn the deduction, you need only maintain an accurate log of your business miles. Multiply the number of business miles by the IRS' standard mileage allowance (it increases each year) to determine the amount of the deduction. If you incur miles for more than one business or activity, I recommend that you maintain two separate logs.

Employee Business Expenses. Ordinary and necessary expenses incurred on behalf of your employer in the performance of your duties as an employee and that are not reimbursed by the employer, may be deducted. A log should provide for such additional expenses as work clothes; safety equipment; education expenses; dues and fees; medical expenses related to your job.

Asset Purchases. Assets placed in use for business may either be depreciated or expensed under section 179. The operator of a small business may not realize purchases of shelving, calculators, etc., used exclusively for the business are deductible assets. If he does know it when the purchase is made, he may forget the fact or the amount of the purchase come tax time. To capture all the deductions, make a log of asset purchases contemporaneously with the purchase. This ensures you claim the full amount of your deduction. An asset purchases log must include the date; check number; type of asset purchased; from whom purchased; whether it was new or used; cost.

Retirement Plan Contributions. A log reflecting deductible payments to an IRA or other retirement plan should be maintained to optimize your deduction. This log must include the date of the contribution; check number; payee; type of plan; nature of the investment; amount.

Itemized Deductions. Itemized deductions are those claimed on Schedule A. They include medical expenses, interest on your principal residence, state and local taxes, charitable contributions and miscellaneous items. A log recording these expenses should be made for each category. Organize the logs as follows: *Medical*--date; payee; check number; prescriptions; doctors; hospitals, etc.; *Taxes*--date; payee; check number; state and local income taxes; real estate taxes; other taxes; *Interest*--date; payee; check number; mortgage interest; deductible points; *Gifts to Charity*--date; payee; check number; cash contributions; non-cash contributions.

A recent amendment to code section 170 requires contemporaneous written acknowledgment by the donee organization of one-time charitable contributions of $250 or more. It is no longer sufficient to rely upon your canceled check as substantiation of a donation of $250 or more. Under the new law, it is incumbent upon you to obtain from the donee organization, i.e., church, etc., a statement verifying the contribution. The substantiation is considered contemporaneous if obtained either before filing the return for the year in question or by the filing due date, including extensions.

The written acknowledgment must contain, 1) the amount of the cash and a description, but not the value, of any property other than cash contributed; 2) whether the organization provided goods or services in return for the contribution; and 3) a description and good-faith estimate of the value of any goods or services provided. If the contributed goods and services consist solely of intangible religious benefits, the acknowledgment must contain a statement to that effect. An "intangible religious benefit" is any benefit provided by an organization organized exclusively for religious purposes and that is not generally sold in a commercial transaction outside the donative context.

As a result of this law, logs are even more necessary. You should include the above information in your log form. It can then be independently verified by your church or other charitable organization. No other method of proof is valid for charitable contributions.

Moving Expenses. Certain moves of your residence can be deductible. If you are planning a move, start by creating a log. That way, all of your moving expenses can be recorded contemporaneously to avoid missing smaller items. A moving expenses log should include the following categories: date; payee; transportation of goods; travel; lodging; temporary living expenses; meals; mileage.

Alimony. Alimony and separate maintenance payments pursuant to a divorce decree or settlement are generally deductible. A log helps to ensure recording all of the expenses as they occur. Such a log must include the date; check number; payee; type of payment; amount.

Miscellaneous or Non-Business Expenses. Expenses not covered above but which are deductible on Schedule A are considered miscellaneous expenses. They include tax preparation, legal fees incurred in connection with audits or other tax disputes, accounting fees and safe deposit box rental.

Adapting these Logs

Each person's facts and circumstances vary. Therefore, employ these logs on a trial basis before making any changes to accommodate your individual needs. After some experience, make whatever alterations are necessary. In my *Smart Tax Forms Kit*, we provide reproducible log blanks for recording both income and expenses. These logs have proven extremely effective for recording both contemporaneous expenses and in reconstructing expenses. The forms kit is a twenty-page booklet containing all the forms mentioned here in reproducible format. It is available from Winning Publications. See ordering information in the back of this book.

Verifying Cash Expenditures

When paying expenses by cash, you always face a potential problem if you do not have a receipt to back them up. Under such circumstances, a contemporaneous log helps greatly but is not guaranteed to work. Cash expenditures for which there is no receipt need verification beyond a contemporaneous log. Testimony must be offered to support such expenses. But when you are not directly questioned concerning those expenses, how do you create testimony to support your claims?

The answer is quite simple. First, maintain your logs on a monthly basis. That is, begin each month with a blank log and new entries. Then, at the close of each month, type a *verification clause* onto your log and have it notarized. The verification clause reads as follows:

The entries in this log were made contemporaneously during the month of _____, (year), and reflect ordinary and necessary expenses of the kind described. Each and every entry in this log is true, correct and complete in all respects and is an accurate reflection of expenses incurred by me (or by _____ business) and paid by check or in cash on the date and for the purpose indicated.

Your Signature

Signature and Seal of Notary

Dated by Notary

When notarized, the log not only provides details of cash expenditures but also provides *contemporaneous sworn testimony* to support it. This procedure eliminates the IRS' capacity to claim the logs are not truthful or accurate or were made in a last minute effort to deceive the agency. Verified logs can then be used to audit-proof your tax return as explained in the next chapter.

In the *Smart Tax Forms Kit*, each of the reproducible log blanks contains a pre-printed verification clause. You need only sign the verification in the presence of a notary public and have the notary sign and seal the log. The verification on income logs should note that all cash received during the period stated is reflected in the log. This contemporaneous record goes a long way to defeat any IRS claim that you had unreported income.

Expanding Logs for Maximum Benefit

The general log forms explained earlier can be expanded to very specific uses. Such uses enable you to accurately record and claim with confidence items you never before claimed. The example I use here relates to charitable contributions. However, specific logs can be applied to any situation where you incur regularly occurring expenses. The focus of these logs is to document cash expenditures simply because most people do not record their cash expenditures in any meaningful way. Thus, otherwise fully deductible expenses fall through the cracks.

Considering specifically the charitable contribution deduction, I heard it said many times one may claim up to $200 in charitable contributions without supporting proof. Stated another way, the theory suggests the IRS simply "gives" you $200 worth of itemized deductions without the need of supporting documentation. This idea is, in a word, nonsense.

The IRS gives you nothing in the way of itemized deductions--charitable or otherwise. If you wish to claim the item, you must prove the legitimacy of the claim through one or more recognized means. By keeping logs of cash expenditures you will no doubt discover the amount you give exceeds $200 per year. Consider the following:

Kiddie Cash. Every small child loves dropping cash into the collection plate on Sunday morning. Often, a quarter or a dollar is handed to the child (or children) just prior to the basket reaching your seat. Once deposited, the money is forgotten. This goes on week after week. If you have just one child, you likely dropped $50 into the collection plate over the course of one year. Now multiply that amount by the number of children you have.

Often parents of older children teach the law of tithing by providing more substantial funds for the child to control and give on his own. Under these circumstances, more substantial amounts are given to your church each Sunday. Based on my own experience as a father of small children, I believe the average family will find an additional $200 to $250 in cash contributions to their church each year.

Before you suggest that recording these transactions is much ado about nothing, consider this. If I freely handed you $100 bill, would you accept it? That is what you stand to gain in tax savings by logging cash contributions of just $250 per year. By using a log in the fashion outlined here, your contributions are unassailable by the IRS and could be worth hundreds of dollars per year in tax savings.

Cookie Cash. How many times have you purchased cookies, candy or some other product from neighborhood children? It may be the Girl Scouts, a playground booster club, a school program or a church fund raiser. Another common solicitation comes in the form of sponsorship requests. You are asked to sponsor a child in the "Walk Against Drugs" or the "Bike Ride for Hope." By agreeing to sponsor a child, you contribute the agreed upon amount, say fifty cents per mile, to the charity promoting the event.

My guess is you donated money to one or more of these causes and you did so in the form of cash. Contributions to these organizations are usually tax-deductible. But there is no way to accurately claim them unless you make a record of the gift at the time it is given.

Create a log and keep it handy. When you make gifts under these circumstances, make a contemporaneous record of the transaction for use at tax return preparation time. You may be entitled to claim an additional $25 or $50 in contributions you otherwise might overlook.

Christmas Cash. Do you give money to the Salvation Army during the Christmas Season? Do you contribute to local food shelves or toy drives? Many millions of citizens across the United States contribute. Just as certainly, those contributions are made largely in cash and the vast majority is not deducted. Just because you give in cash does not mean you cannot deduct the contribution. The contribution is deductible whether given in cash or not. However, you must prove you gave the cash.

Keep a log of cash contributions. Include not only the coins dropped in collection pots but the canned corn donated to the food shelf. Have your contribution acknowledged by the charity if it exceeds $250.

Clothes Cash. Do you dispose of used clothing or other household items by conducting a garage sale? Or, do you donate them to the Salvation Army, Goodwill or your own church rummage sale? If you donate them to any of the latter causes, your contribution is tax deductible.

Unfortunately, millions of citizens who do contribute goods to charity do not claim the benefits they are entitled to. Folks regularly unload boxes of used clothing at Goodwill centers without bothering to create a log of the items contributed. Your log should list the specific items donated together with a declaration of their fair market value on the date of the gift. Have your list signed by a representative of the charity to whom given. The organization does not verify the value of the items, merely that it received what you gave. Make sure the signed statement meets the requirements discussed above to constitute an acknowledgment of the contribution. The log constitutes proof of the contribution.

Creating Specialty Logs

Each of the logs discussed thus far is pointed at recording very objective occurrences: the expenditure of a sum of money on a specific item for some particular purpose. However, the deductibility of many business expenses depends not only on the amount of the expenditure--an *objective* consideration--but the business purpose of the expenditure--something entirely *subjective*. One person's view of what constitutes a necessary business expense is not always in agreement with the next person's (a tax auditor, for example) view.

Now add the fact that the deductibility of certain expenses is dependent upon *intangible* aspects. For example, your ability to deduct a portion of your home as office expenses depends largely upon whether your home office space is used "regularly and exclusively" for business purposes. The so-called "exclusive use" test is an intangible item because under no circumstances can you obtain written evidence to prove "exclusive use." You cannot, for example, obtain a receipt from your children indicating they are not allowed to play in the den.

Thus, safely proving your entitlement to a home office deduction necessitates the use of specialty logs. When employing such logs in other areas, you greatly increase the scope and value of your business deductions. Consider these items:

The Home Office. The tax code allows a deduction for a home office when a portion of the home is used regularly and exclusively as the principle place of business. The space used for the office is deductible when you regularly meet with customers, clients or patients or when it is used to perform administrative and managerial tasks associated with the business and there is no other fixed location of your business in which to perform those tasks.

A log evidencing the use of your home office is vitally important. It alone enables you to prove what you are doing in your home office and whether you meet with customers on a regular basis. Without such a log, you have little chance of prevailing in your claim for a home office deduction.

The home office log is completed on a daily basis. The log has columns for each of the following entries: date; task performed; name of client/customer. Describe in general terms the administrative or managerial tasks you performed and whether you met with a customer or client. For each task performed, list the date and a general description of the job.

The Home Computer. Many people purchase home computers for use in a mix of business and personal reasons but do not claim the deduction. I find the IRS challenging the deduction of home computers because citizens often lack the proof needed to establish the business use of the machine. You may ask, "How does one prove business use of a computer?" The answer is, with a log.

A log dedicated to equipment usage allows you to make a record each time you use your computer. (Why not computerize it?) The log reflects the date of use; the function performed; whether business or personal; the time spent. After maintaining the log for a thirty-day period, you can ascertain the percentage of time spent on business functions.

The percentage of business use established over the entire tax year determines the deductible percentage of the total cost of the computer. For example, suppose your logs reveal you spend 65 percent of your home computer time performing business related functions. If you paid $2,000 for your computer, you are entitled to a business deduction of $1,300 ($2,000 x .65 = $1,300). The key to establishing the deduction is to keep the log. Only with the log are you able to unequivocally prove 65 percent business use of the home computer.

Other Business Equipment. The above idea is not limited to personal computers. Any piece of equipment that has at least some business use is subject to the allocation formula mentioned. Remember that you do not have to be self-employed to claim these deductions. If you purchase equipment for use in your job and are not reimbursed by your employer, you may be able to claim a deduction for the expense on Form 2106, *Employee*

Business Expenses. Do not be afraid to make logs covering the following:

1) Video Cassette Recorder. Many people employed in direct marking companies use VCRs to make sales presentations. Make a log using precisely the same form illustrated for the computer. Indicate at the top of the log which item it covers.

2) Telephone use. Be sure to note whether the call was long distance. Long distance business phone calls are not subject to any allocation rule. If the call has a business purpose, it may be deductible. Record business use on a log.

3) FAX use. With a fax machine used partially for business purposes, a log enables you to deduct the correct percentage as a business expense.

Meals and Entertainment. Entertainment expenses must be given careful consideration. The reason is the IRS and Congress have established stringent rules for deductibility of such expenses. Earlier in the discussion, I touched on the rules but let us elaborate.

Entertainment and meals are deductible when they constitute an ordinary and necessary business expenses, and they are 1) directly related to the operation of your business, or 2) they directly precede or follow a bona fide and substantial business discussion.

The entertainment can take place at a restaurant, sporting event, theater or other non-business environment. The entertainment can be for the benefit of existing or potential clients or customers, suppliers, dealers, professional counsel or employees.

The key to the deductibility of any meal or entertainment expense is a log. The log must carefully note the persons entertained, the business purpose of the entertainment, the bona fide and substantial business discussion that took place either before, during or after the entertainment, the date and of course, the amount of the expense.

Proper logs carry your meal and entertainment expense deduction well beyond the charge card slips we generally fall back on. Consider the following:

Entertaining at Home. When you conduct bona fide and substantial business meetings in your home, the cost of entertainment associated with such meetings is deductible. Your log must record the date of the entertainment, the persons in attendance and their affiliation to your business, the purpose of the entertainment and a description of the substantial and bona fide discussions had either before, during or after the gathering. The purpose of the entertainment must be commercial and not merely social. You must have records of the costs of food, beverages, etc., served at the gathering. The *Smart Tax Forms Kit* contains two reproducible log forms that satisfy the reporting requirements for this deduction.

Entertainment Facilities. You may already know it is not legal to deduct the cost of maintaining or operating so-called "entertainment facilities." Entertainment facilities include boats, vacation homes, swimming pools, etc. However, it is possible, under the rules discussed above, to deduct entertainment expenses incurred while using those facilities. Entertainment expenses include food, beverages, supplies, etc., related to providing business entertainment at or with the facility.

For example, if you own a boat, the cost of maintaining and operating the boat is not deductible. However, if you entertain business associates on your boat from time to time, the cost of such entertainment (apart from operating the boat) is deductible. Those costs include the food, beverages, etc., supplied for the entertainment. You must maintain logs just as you would for home entertainment. The logs must reveal the same information as shown under *Entertaining at Home.*

Conclusion

I know this seems like a lot of recordkeeping but remember what I said earlier. Not every person is going to use all these logs. Use only those that apply to you. Also remember that the lack of proper records is what usually enables the IRS to take unfair advantage of citizens. However, when you properly understand your burden with regard to the tax return, you are in a better position to *assert* deductions than any agent is in to *deny* them.

CHAPTER TEN
Audit-Proof and Penalty-Proof Your Tax Return

Each year, the IRS audits 100 percent of the income returns filed. The audit process is accomplished largely through electronic means with computers performing the task. In addition to the electronic audits, approximately 2 percent of all individual tax returns are subjected to a face-to-face audit examination. The idea of such an examination is terrifying to most people.

On the mind of each citizen about to file his tax return is the question, "How do I avoid an audit?" The answer offered by too many tax experts over the years always disturbs me. Professional preparers often suggest that one fail to claim various deductions to which he is entitled. The theory is that by doing so, he reduces the chances of being selected for examination. Stated another way, the prevailing "professional" opinion is one should *buy* audit protection by ignoring legitimate deductions.

As already stated, this has the direct effect of raising your tax bill. Another oft-cited "professional" technique for limiting the potential bite of an audit requires one to hold back deduction items at the time of filing. The theory is if audited, those items can later be thrown on the table to negate the effect of any disallowed deductions. This too amounts to the purchase of audit protection insurance at the price of increased taxes.

The IRS' audit statistics reveal that neither of these techniques is at all sound. In the first place, the IRS' computers examine 100 percent of all returns filed. There is nothing anybody can do to prevent that. Merely failing to claim legitimate deductions does nothing to preclude that scrutiny. Secondly, IRS claims that about 88 percent of all citizens audited are found to owe more money. The average amount due after face-to-face examination is more than $4,500 that doubles with penalties and interest. Therefore, the tactic of holding back deductions at the time of filing, only to spring them on the auditor later, simply does not work.

Both of the foregoing techniques for avoiding an audit are based upon two fundamental misunderstandings. The first is uncertainty about how returns are selected for audit. Second are misgivings about what it means to be audited. Here, we examine both questions. Ultimately, we answer--once and for all--what can be done to avoid being dragged through the hot coals of a face-to-face tax audit *without* losing one dime of deductions in the process. These techniques allow one to claim with confidence all legitimate deductions.

Lastly, a valuable byproduct of my recordkeeping and returns filing technique is the introduction of a new level of financial privacy. Following these techniques enables you to rest assured you have met your legal obligation to prove the correctness of your tax return. At the same time, you minimize the extent to which you must bear your financial soul to the IRS. Truly, this system allows you to close the IRS' spying eyes in its attempt to criticize each detail of your financial affairs.

How Returns are Selected for Audit

None of what I say in the following pages means anything unless you understand how the IRS selects returns for audit. After you learn the audit selection basics, you can more fully appreciate how my audit-proofing techniques operate. The IRS uses several basic techniques to select tax returns for audit. Let us briefly address each of them.

Mathematical Errors. Upon receiving a return, service center computers compare all computations for mathematical accuracy. Upon finding an error, the computer generates a correction notice, then mails it to the citizen. The notice demands payment of the additional taxes, with penalties and interest. Each year, IRS generates millions of these notices. I have documented, both in my writing and in testimony before House and Senate tax committees, that these notices are wrong about half the time. See *IRS, Taxes and the Beast,* chapter four, for more details.

Mechanical Errors. The same computers search for mechanical errors in return preparation. Such errors might include failure to attach a necessary supporting schedule or failure to carry a total from a schedule to the tax return itself. When such errors are detected, correction notices are mailed to the citizen.

Unreported Income. The IRS operates a program known as the Information Returns Program in which computers compare all information returns filed (Forms 1099 and W-2) with all tax returns. If the computer reveals the presence of an information return showing payment of income but such income is not reported on a tax return, the computer issues a correction notice. The notice adds the unreported income to the return then computes the additional tax due. In turn, it demands payment of the additional tax, with interest and penalties.

The Information Returns Program is designed to detect non-filers in the same manner. For example, suppose the computer detects a Form W-2 showing receipt of $20,000 in wages. However, in cross-checking for a tax return, it finds none was filed for the year in question. You are considered a non-filer and are mailed a notice demanding you file a return or explain why none was filed. If you fail, IRS computes your tax liability based on available information and bills you accordingly.

The Discriminate Function. The Discriminate Function System, known as the DIF system, is a sophisticated computer program that compares each entry of your tax return with national and regional statistical averages for persons in your same income category and profession. If any line of your return is out of sync with those averages, the difference is scored. It is known as a DIF score. The higher the score, the greater the likelihood of an audit. The vast majority of all returns selected for audit are selected using the DIF program.

The DIF program is the system that the typical audit-proofing guidance is designed to beat. Theoretically, if one merely reduces the amount of deductions claimed, those remaining fall below the averages. That way, he is assured his return will not be selected for examination.

There are two distinct problems with this theory. First, nobody knows the DIF thresholds and the IRS will not release them. Therefore, any effort to place your claims below those scores is purely speculative. Secondly, even if we did know them, in order to place yourself below the threshold, you must forego claiming deductions you are lawfully entitled to claim. This is like throwing the baby out with the bath water.

Furthermore, the philosophy behind the typical audit-proofing techniques is all wrong. Those who exercise the practice of reducing claims in order to avoid an audit do not understand an audit. The audit is nothing more than the process by which the IRS determines the correctness of a tax return. The fact that your return may be selected for audit is no indication whatsoever that there is an *error* in the return.

Rather, the selection indicates only that there is a *question* raised by one or more claims in the return. The audit is the process by which IRS obtains answers to those questions. Provided you are able to demonstrate the accuracy of your return and you understand your rights, the audit holds absolutely no hidden danger or financial risk. For more details on audit section, defense and audit appeal procedures, see *IRS, Taxes and the Beast*.

How My System Works

How can we take what we know about the audit selection process and use it to audit-proof a tax return? The answer lies partially with recordkeeping logs. We know the IRS selects the vast majority of returns for audit, not based upon known errors in the returns but based upon its statistical variance with stated parameters.

I know from studying the IRS' audit referral system that returns selected by the DIF program are first assigned to a reviewer at the service center. Only after a reviewer finds a need for a face-to-face exam is the return formally referred to the local district for an audit. My audit-proofing techniques are designed to take effect at the point of service center review. When successful, the techniques prevent the return from being forwarded for full-scale exam. The result is you avoid the hassle, anxiety and trauma of a face-to-face audit--not to mention the $4,500 tax bill that accompanies it.

I know from experience that when sufficient information is provided with the return *at the time of filing*, there is no need to forward the return for full-scale examination. Therefore, we effectively short-circuit the audit process by simply providing sufficient information with the return at the time of filing. The information must answer any potential questions raised by the return itself.

Let me offer an example. Suppose your logs reveal you are entitled to claim 20,000 business miles during the year. Suppose further, however, your tax professional or your inner voice advises you that claiming 20,000 business miles will raise a red flag. Rather than reduce your claim to something less, my techniques allow you to claim the full amount of the deduction and do it without risk.

To audit-proof the claim, make a copy of your verified mileage log and attach the copy (never send originals) directly to the tax return at the time of filing. In this fashion, you have both claimed every deduction you are entitled to claim and have provided information with the return sufficient to answer any potential questions regarding the claim. If the DIF program because of the apparently high mileage claim kicks out your return, IRS service center reviewers find attached to the return all information needed to verify your claim. At that point, the matter is not pursued further.

Keep in mind, over 200 million personal and business tax returns are filed each year. At the same time, just 2 percent are assigned for face-to-face examination. Which returns do you suppose the IRS wishes to spend its limited time auditing, your documented return or one of the millions of undocumented returns?

Do you wish to be absolutely safe concerning all claims on your return? If so, audit-proof each and every deduction. Complete audit-proofing is done not just by providing copies of your verified logs. Indeed, the logs are a means of enabling you to capture all of your expenses, particularly those that generally fall through the cracks. But there is more. Full-scale audit-proofing is accomplished by attaching to your return copies of all information necessary to prove a claim. This includes logs, canceled checks, cash receipts and year-end statements.

A fully audit-proofed return provides copies of all the information that otherwise is provided to a tax auditor in a face-to-face environment. In this manner, you completely eliminate the need to see an auditor, even if there is an incorrect claim on the return. You and the IRS may act strictly through the mail. Since you provide all documentation and details with your return, a face-to-face meeting is unnecessary. This is consistent with the right to a so-called correspondence audit. In a correspondence audit, you never enter the lion's den. Rather, you operate out of your home or office and through the mail. For more on the correspondence audit, see *IRS, Taxes and the Beast*.

To summarize, a properly audit-proofed return contains the following attachments:

1. An explanation of the nature of the claim. Use IRS Form 8275, *Disclosure Statement*, for this purpose. I like to refer to Form 8275 as the audit-proof form because it provides the basis of your audit-proofing package. An example of Form 8275 is shown on the next two pages and a reproducible copy is found in our *Forms Kit*.

2. A complete explanation of the purpose of the expense (if a business expense, your explanation should include a statement as to why the expense is "ordinary and necessary" to the operation of your business);

3. Copies of all documentary evidence available to support the deduction, including logs; and

4. If the IRS has a particular form covering the deduction, such as Form 4684 for Casualty and Theft Losses, or Form 8283 for Non-Cash Charitable Contributions, complete the form and attach it to the return.

When a return is documented with this kind of proof, you eliminate the need for an audit. Even beyond that, should a claim be disallowed for some reason, you avoid being penalized. The

Form **8275**		**Disclosure Statement**			OMB No. 1545-0889
(Rev. March 1998)		Do not use this form to disclose items or positions that are contrary to Treasury regulations. Instead, use Form 8275-R, Regulation Disclosure Statement. See separate instructions.			
Department of the Treasury Internal Revenue Service		▶ Attach to your tax return.			Attachment Sequence No **92**
Name(s) shown on return					Identifying number shown on return

Part I   General Information (see instructions)

(a) Rev. Rul., Rev. Proc., etc.	(b) Item or Group of Items	(c) Detailed Description of Items	(d) Form or Schedule	(e) Line No.	(f) Amount
1					
2					
3					

Part II   Detailed Explanation (see instructions)

1

2

3

Part III   Information About Pass-Through Entity. To be completed by partners, shareholders, beneficiaries, or residual interest holders.

Complete this part only if you are making adequate disclosure for a pass-through item.

Note: *A pass-through entity is a partnership, S corporation, estate, trust, regulated investment company, real estate investment trust, or real estate mortgage investment conduit (REMIC).*

1 Name, address, and ZIP code of pass-through entity	2 Identifying number of pass-through entity
	3 Tax year of pass-through entity to
	4 Internal Revenue Service Center where the pass-through entity filed its return

For Paperwork Reduction Act Notice, see separate instructions.   Form **8275** (Rev 3-98)
ISA
STF FED0518F.1

Form 8275 (Rev 3-98)   Page **2**

Part IV	Explanations *(continued from Parts I and/or II)*

reason is when "full disclosure" of all facts, supporting documents and reasonable justification for the claim are presented with the return, the law does not permit the IRS to assess penalties. A case study illustrates my point.

The case is that of *Stein v. Commissioner*, T.C. Memo. 1992-651 (Nov. 5, 1992). In 1988, Hester received a lump sum distribution of $44,000 from her employer. The distribution was part of an early retirement incentive package. According to documents provided by the employer, the source of the distribution was a pension plan. Both Hester and her employer believed the distribution did not constitute severance pay.

When the employer issued a W-2, however, it identified the $44,000 distribution as *wage income*. On her 1988 tax return, however, Hester did not treat the distribution as wage income. Rather, she called it a *pension distribution*. She elected to income average the payment over ten years as allowed by law at the time.

On the face of her Form 1040, Hester added this language, "Lump sum Distribution erroneously reported by employer on W-2 and reportable on Form 4972 (relating to pension distributions)." In addition, she attached to the return a copy of a statement prepared and issued by the employer. It described the payment plainly as a pension distribution.

The IRS determined that Hester in fact received severance pay, not a pension distribution. As it turned out, the agency was right according to the fine print in her contract. She should have reported the payment as wage income not subject to the ten-year income averaging right. As a result, she owed more income tax. However, the IRS' claim did not end there. IRS ordered Hester to pay the sum of $2,244 as a penalty under code section 6662.

Hester challenged the penalty. She claimed she was not liable for a penalty because she made full disclosure to the IRS of the facts surrounding her claim on the face of return. The IRS was on notice of the nature of her claim. At the time of filing, she provided documentation sufficient to allow the IRS pass upon its merits.

Revenue Regulation 1.6662-4(b)(1) provides that disclosure is adequate if a statement is attached to the return which includes, a) a caption identifying the statement as a section 6662 disclosure, b) identification of the item to which disclosure is made, c) the amount of the item in question, and d) the facts affecting the tax treatment of the item that reasonably may be expected to apprise the IRS of the nature of the potential controversy concerning the tax treatment of the item.

The IRS has a form that meets all those requirements. I referred to it earlier as the audit-proof form but it also penalty-proofs the return. It is Form 8275, *Disclosure Statement,* a copy of which is reproduced above. In this case, Hester *did not* use Form 8275. Rather, she simply added an explanation to the return and attached supporting documentation. The IRS argued that her failure to use the form meant the $2,244 penalty should apply. The Tax Court rejected the argument, saying:

> (Hester) did not use Form 8275. Yet, our inquiry does not end there. According to the Joint Committee's (Joint Committee on Taxation, US Congress) explanation of section 6662, "disclosure is adequate if the taxpayer discloses facts sufficient to enable the IRS to identify the potential controversy, if it analyzed that information."

After analyzing Hester's disclosure, the court held:

> We conclude that the disclosure on (Hester's) return was adequate to disclose the controversy. (Hester) did not try to hide the position she had taken on her 1988 tax return as is often done by those attempting the "audit lottery." (Hester) not only made a notation on the tax return that indicated the position she had taken, but also attached a copy of the explanation of the payment which indicated the potential controversy. We, therefore, hold that (Hester) is not subject to the (penalty) under section 6662.

In this case, Hester saved $2,244 by penalty-proofing her tax return as I suggest. While she did not use Form 8275, her effort was nevertheless successful. The key to avoiding penalties is simple. Do not attempt to hide your claim from the IRS. When making a potentially controversial claim, disclose the facts to the IRS, allowing it to pass upon the merits of the claim. By doing so, if it transpires you are not entitled to the tax treatment elected, as was the case with Hester's distribution, you avoid the penalties associated with the claim.

You may be thinking that Form 8275 is a way to call attention to yourself. "Why file the form," you ask, "if all it does is trigger an audit?" The form itself does not trigger an audit. An audit is triggered when the computer flags a potential trouble spot in your return. More pointedly, the DIF scores trigger the audit. By not using Form 8275, you are virtually assured the return will be handed off for a face-to-face examination if a complex or questionable item appears.

By using Form 8275 and providing supporting documentation as outlined here, you are assured there is no need for face-to-face scrutiny. By providing supporting material with the return, IRS need only pass upon the merits of your claim. That is exactly what happened in Hester's case. Of course, if IRS disallows your deduction, you have the right to appeal the decision. The important key is, even if you lose on the merits of the deduction, you *prevent the assessment of very costly penalties.* In Hester's case, the extra few minutes she spent penalty-proofing saved exactly $2,244.

A New Wrinkle in Penalty-Proofing Requirements

Penalties are big business for the IRS. Each year, the agency assesses over thirty million penalties against individuals and businesses, netting over $10 billion in revenue. During the 1990s, penalties have been used by Congress and the administration as a "revenue enhancement" tool. No longer are they considered a mere deterrence to abhorrent taxpayer behavior. They are intended as a means to collect more money.

One congressional amendment altered code sections 6662 and 6694 expressly to allow for the collection of more penalty revenue. Under the old law, one avoided a penalty if his position was disclosed on the return as outlined above *and* if the position was not "frivolous." A position is "frivolous" only if it is "patently improper." See Revenue Regulations, sec. 1.6662-3(b)(3). A claim that is arguable--whether or not correct--but not patently improper, is not "frivolous."

Congress tightened the belt on this rule. Under the current law, you avoid penalties only if your position has "at least a reasonable basis" for the claim. This standard is *higher* than the not "frivolous" standard described above. The Conference Committee reporting the change describes the difference in these terms:

> The conferees intend that "reasonable basis" be a relatively high standard of tax reporting, that is, significantly higher than "not patently improper." This standard is not satisfied by a return position which is merely arguable or that is merely a colorable claim. Conference report, H.R. 2264, August 4, 1993, page 205.

In light of this, the disclosure aspect of penalty-proofing remains critical. In addition, you must be able to demonstrate that your position has a *reasonable basis* in law and fact. This standard requires one to exercise some due diligence prior to making any potentially troublesome claim. That is, you must make a reasonable effort to ascertain the correctness of your claim before asserting it. Provided you discover sufficient evidence to persuade a reasonable person as to the correctness of the claim, the penalty is avoided if the claim is properly disclosed to the IRS and supported as shown above.

Affidavits as an Audit- and Penalty-Proofing Tool

Affidavits play an important role in the audit-proofing and penalty-proofing scenario. There are some cases in which the propriety of a deduction turns on information that cannot be provided through documentation obtained from a third party. This is what I referred to earlier as an "intangible" element of the deduction. Such information is just as essential to proving the deduction but must be presented in another fashion.

For example, a home office claim is acceptable only if the space in the home is used "regularly and exclusively for business purposes." No deduction is allowed when office space is used for personal, non-business purposes such as an evening TV room. Thus, proof must be presented in the form of testimony to establish the "intangible" element of business use.

Achieve the task by using an affidavit. An affidavit is nothing more than a sworn statement presenting detailed facts. The statement becomes testimony when the affidavit is notarized. Testimony proves the truth of the matter asserted when it is plausible, believable and uncontroverted.

Of course, unless you are an outright tax criminal, the IRS generally does not offer evidence to refute your claims. In short, it simply does not have to. You must prove that your return is correct and complete. If you are unable to do this for any reason, you lose without the IRS lifting a finger. That is what makes an affidavit so effective. The agency rarely, if ever, refutes it with evidence to the contrary.

In the home office example, an affidavit must unequivocally declare that the office space is used regularly and exclusively for business purposes. It should state that no personal, non-business use occurs within the space. To be effective, one must also establish that he meets all other home office elements as well. We addressed those in previous chapters.

For further details on the use and preparation of affidavits, see my book *41 Ways to Lick the IRS with a Postage Stamp*, chapters three and four.

An Increased Measure of Financial Privacy

With all its ability to demand the production of information, it is difficult to understand how anybody has any degree of financial privacy remaining vis-à-vis the IRS. The truth is, measured against the yardstick of what may be considered constitutional standards, we have little or no financial privacy. The IRS' ability to demand records, access your bank account and obtain data from other third parties makes true financial privacy a thing of the past.

But the procedures outlined in chapters nine and ten of this book restore some measure of privacy. It is ironic to believe that creating detailed records in some capacity restores what was once a cherished right. Nevertheless, it is true. Bear in mind your legal burden of proof with regard to the claims made in your return. You must prove the correctness of all claims regarding income and expenses. If you claim to have earned $15,000 income, you must show the claim to be accurate. If you claim to have incurred $5,000 in charitable contribution deductions, you must prove the accuracy of that claim as well.

It is important to understand the limits of the IRS' reach in this regard. The agency has the right to demand proof of any item claimed in the return. However, its power does not extend beyond that point. Stated another way, the IRS has no authority to delve into every aspect of your financial life if those issues have no bearing upon the correctness of your tax return.

For example, if you make no claim of any charitable deduction, the IRS has no right to question you regarding your charitable giving. This distinction is important because during the course of a typical audit, agents routinely demand the production of a myriad of documents. This is especially true in the economic reality audit in which the IRS tries to uncover every aspect of your private life. The agency generally seeks all canceled checks, bank deposit slips, monthly bank statements, documents concerning loans and repayments of such loans, and on and on. But if these issues have no bearing upon the truthfulness of the claims in your return, they are entirely irrelevant.

A clear example arises with regard to the demand for "all canceled checks." If you were to examine the checks written during the course of an average month, you would find payments for groceries, haircuts, recreational activity, restaurants, car payments, gasoline, day care, theater tickets, maybe even a parking ticket, etc., etc., etc.

The point is, the vast majority of the expenses you incur in a given month are of a personal nature and are non-deductible. Moreover, unless you are a tax criminal, I suspect you made no effort to deduct such expenses.

Consequently, the nature, amount and purpose of such expenses are simply of *no legitimate concern* to the IRS. Stated more pointedly, it is *none of their business* how you spend your money on non-deductible expenses. The agency therefore has no right to demand and you are under no obligation to produce records which have no bearing upon issues raised in the return.

This reality no doubt closes the door on much more than 50 percent of what the IRS demands to see. By using the audit-proof and penalty-proof techniques outlined here, what it has a right to see is readily organized, easily understood and probably already provided with the return. Under such circumstances, the agency has no legitimate claim to more information.

Using these techniques eliminates the need to sift through every document you own to respond to a steady stream of IRS demands. In fact, it likely eliminates the need to deal with an auditor altogether because the documentation necessary to prove the claims in the return was submitted with the return. Provided you did so, you enjoy the legitimate right and power to say "no" to further demands.

In essence, you have the right to terminate an audit when it exceeds the legal limits. You have the right to stop an agent from prying or attempting to pry into issues that have no bearing upon the correctness of the return. You have the right to assert your financial privacy and can make it stick when adequately prepared. Indeed, if you do not assert that right, you surely will enjoy no right of financial privacy. To be sure, the IRS portends no limits to its own power.

While this right certainly exists, few exercise it because they are afraid of the power of the tax auditor. The truth be told, tax auditors have no power. As I examine more closely in *IRS, Taxes and the Beast*, auditors operate largely on tactics of bluff and intimidation. They employ misinformation and disinformation. Often, they overtly lie concerning audit issues, taxpayer obligations and potential consequences. When you understand these facts, you become more willing and able to exercise your rights. Your right of privacy naturally grows as a result.

Glossary

90%/100% RULE: The rule that requires one to make ESTIMATED PAYMENTS equal to either 90 percent of the current TAX LIABILITY or 100 percent the prior year's tax liability, whichever is less.

401(k) PLAN: An employer-sponsored retirement plan under which employees are allowed to defer income and employers may make non-taxable matching contributions.

ABATEMENT: The administrative process of canceling a tax or penalty.

APPEALS OFFICE: An office within the IRS established to hear taxpayer challenges to IRS decisions.

ASSESSMENT: The administrative process the IRS follows of recording a tax liability as an official debt. Once making the assessment, the IRS may use its enforcement tools to collect.

AUDIT-PROOFING: The process of providing information with the tax return that answers all potential questions raised in the return.

CAFETERIA PLAN: An employer-sponsored plan under which employees are offered a series of benefits from which they pick and choose. The benefits could include child care, medical care, dental care, etc. See FLEXIBLE SPENDING ARRANGEMENT and SALARY REDUCTION AGREEMENT.

COLLECTION APPEAL: An appeals process codified by the IRS RESTRUCTURING AND REFORM ACT under which a citizen may challenge any IRS collection action, including wage levies, bank levies, tax liens and property seizures. See APPEALS OFFICE.

CONTEMPORANEOUS RECORDS: Records that are made at the time the event being recorded occurs. Examples are mileage records made at the time of the travel. See LOGS.

DISCRIMINATE FUNCTION SYSTEM (DIF): The IRS computer program responsible for selecting returns for audit. The DIF program compares each line of a tax return with national and regional statistical averages then scores the difference. The higher the variance from the averages, the greater the likelihood of an audit.

EARNED INCOME TAX CREDIT: A credit against taxes offered to those with both dependent children and low to moderate income. See FORM W-5.

ECONOMIC REALITY AUDIT: An IRS audit program that focuses upon lifestyle as a means of discovering alleged unreported income.

EDUCATION IRA: A non-deductible savings program that allows parents to invest money for their children's education. The money grows tax-free and may be withdrawn tax-free provided it is used for qualified education expenses. See INDIVIDUAL RETIREMENT ACCOUNT.

EFFECTIVE TAX RATE: The rate of tax one pays after computing the benefit of all deductions, allowances, exemptions and credits.

ESTIMATED PAYMENTS: Periodic tax payments made during the course of the year as advance payments against the yet undetermined tax liability.

EXEMPTION: A deduction from gross income based upon one's dependents.

FLEXIBLE SPENDING ARRANGEMENT (FSA): Part of a package of benefits offered to employees by their employer. Usually, the FSA is offered as a part of a CAFETERIA PLAN and SALARY REDUCTION AGREEMENT.

FORM W-2: Wage and Tax Statement--An INFORMATION RETURN filed by your employer with the IRS on which your gross income and total tax withholdings is reported.

FORM W-4: Employee's Withholding Allowance Certificate--filed by employees with their employers on which they declare the number of WITHHOLDING ALLOWANCES they are entitled to for purposes of calculating the amount of federal income tax withheld from their paycheck.

FORM W-5: Earned Income Credit Advance Payment Certificate--The form filed with one's employer for the purposes of claiming advance payment of the EARNED INCOME TAX CREDIT.

FORM 1099: Miscellaneous Income--An INFORMATION RETURN used to report payments to the IRS for services when such services are not performed by an employee. Other payments, such as dividends, interest and royalties are reported using FORM 1099.

INDEPENDENT CONTRACTOR: A self-employed person who performs services for any number of others, including both individuals and businesses.

INDIVIDUAL RETIREMENT ACCOUNT (IRA): A retirement plan established by an individual person, apart from his employer, to which he makes tax deductible contributions and which contributions grow tax-deferred until withdrawn.

INFORMATION RETURN: A document submitted to the IRS reporting information only, such as FORM 1099 and FORM W-2.

INFORMATION RETURNS PROGRAM: A computer program that cross-checks all FORMS 1099 and W-2 with tax returns to determine whether all income reported on the INFORMATION RETURNS is declared on the tax returns.

INTERNAL REVENUE CODE: The federal tax law as passed by Congress.

INTERNAL REVENUE MANUAL (IRM): The IRS' guidebook written for its agents and employees to guide them in the conduct of their official duties.

INTERNAL REVENUE REGULATIONS: The administrative rules written by the IRS to implement the INTERNAL REVENUE CODE.

INTERNAL REVENUE SERVICE RESTRUCTURING AND REFORM ACT OF 1998: The major tax reform act passed by Congress effective July 22, 1998.

LOGS: The tool used to keep CONTEMPORANEOUS RECORDS of various expenses and activities, such as mileage, entertainment, etc.

MEDICAL SAVINGS ACCOUNT (MSA): An account to which one may make tax deductible contributions for the purpose of paying medical expenses not covered by insurance.

OVER-WITHHOLDING: The process of allowing one's employer to withhold too much money from his paycheck, leading to a tax refund. See UNDER-WITHHOLDING.

PERCENTAGE METHOD OF WITHHOLDING: One of two approved methods of determining the amount of money to be withheld from one's paycheck. It is based upon a percentage of one's income after considering the WITHHOLDING ALLOWANCES to which he is entitled. See WAGE BRACKET METHOD OF WITHHOLDING.

RECONSTRUCTIONS: Expense calculations that are rebuilt after original records are lost or destroyed.

ROTH IRA: A hybrid IRA under which one is not allowed to deduct contributions to the IRA but from which he may make tax-free withdrawals after reaching age 59½. See INDIVIDUAL RETIREMENT ACCOUNT.

SALARY REDUCTION AGREEMENT: A written agreement between an employer and his employees under which employees are allowed to pay for fringe benefits from their gross pay and which benefits are not subject to income tax. See CAFETERIA PLAN and FLEXIBLE SPENDING ARRANGEMENT.

SAVINGS INCENTIVE MATCH PLAN FOR EMPLOYEES (SIMPLE): An employer-sponsored retirement plan that allows for tax deductible contributions to be made to a tax-deferred pension. See INDIVIDUAL RETIREMENT ACCOUNT and 401(k) PLAN.

SELF-DIRECTED IRA: An IRA held by an independent trustee giving the owner control over the manner in which the proceeds are invested. See INDIVIDUAL RETIREMENT ACCOUNT.

SELF-EMPLOYMENT TAXES: SOCIAL SECURITY TAXES calculated on the profit of a self-employed person.

SIMPLIFIED EMPLOYEE PENSION (SEP): An employee pension plan sponsored by an employer that allows for tax deductible contributions to be made to a tax-deferred pension. See INDIVIDUAL RETIREMENT ACCOUNT and 401(k) PLAN.

SOCIAL SECURITY TAXES: An income tax equal to 15.3 percent of gross income. Employees pay 7.65 percent and employers must match that. Self-employed persons pay the entire 15.3 percent based upon their profit. See SELF-EMPLOYMENT TAX.

TAX LIABILITY: The debt for taxes owed to the IRS.

TAXPAYER ADVOCATE: An administrative office within the IRS the function of which is to act as a liaison between the IRS and the citizen for the purpose of solving problems when normal IRS channels fail.

TRUSTEE: One who has fiduciary responsibility over the assets of another.

UNDER-WITHHOLDING: The process of allowing one's employer to withhold too little money from his paycheck, leading to a tax liability. See OVER-WITHHOLDING.

WAGE BRACKET METHOD OF WITHHOLDING: One of two approved methods of determining the amount of money to be withheld from one's paycheck. It is based upon a series of WITHHOLDING TABLES that take into account one's income after considering his WITHHOLDING ALLOWANCES. See PERCENTAGE METHOD OF WITHHOLDING.

WITHHOLDING ALLOWANCE: A claim on FORM W-4 that affects the amount of withholding from one's paycheck. The more allowances claimed, the less is withheld for federal income tax purposes.

WITHHOLDING TABLES: Extensive charts found within IRS Circular E which show at a glance the amount of withholding one is to receive based upon his filing status, WITHHOLDING ALLOWANCES, pay period and gross income.

DAN PILLA'S
COMPLETE IRS DEFENSE LIBRARY

41 Ways To Lick the IRS With a Postage Stamp...

Contains perhaps the most comprehensive discussion of IRS Penalty Abatement Procedures of any book ever written. You can even abate interest in certain cases where IRS error or delay is the cause of mounting tax bills. It is written for the average taxpayer and includes over forty sample letters you can use to abate penalties and enforce your rights.

Within this book you find sample affidavits and the secrets to using them with the IRS' own audit-proofing forms. Now you can get out of trouble and stay out of trouble with the IRS. This book is proof that the pen is truly mightier than the sword!

...$15.95 plus P&H

IRS, Taxes and the Beast...

In 1984, IRS began to implement its secret "Strategic Plan," the goal of which is to audit every citizen each year. Claiming 80% of citizens cheat on their taxes by underreporting income, IRS relies more and more on computers to monitor all financial transactions. Financial Privacy is about to become something written of only in history books.

As computers scan more and more financial records, more people are sucked into the audit machine, a machine that grinds you up unless you know the limit of IRS power. This book is a complete audit defense guide designed to help you avoid the pitfalls brought on by ignorance of your rights. It includes dozens of tips and techniques for surviving audits and maintaining a higher level of financial privacy and freedom.

...$15.95 plus P&H

Taxpayers' Ultimate Defense Manual...

When your rights have been violated and you have already paid taxes you do not owe, you need to call out the biggest defensive weapons we have in our arsenal. Sometimes the best offense is a great defense. This book provides you with nine different Actions, Petitions, Procedures and even Lawsuits you can use to defend your wealth and your rights! On the next page is a list of all the actions you can take without the high cost of legal assistance.

Actions, Petitions, Procedures and Lawsuits

- Using Tax Court to Call the Final IRS Bluff
- Recover Illegally Seized Property
- Make the IRS Pay Your Cost of Fighting When They Lose
- Claim a Refund On Past Returns
- Protect the Assets of an Innocent Spouse
- Punish IRS Agents for Unlawful Collection Activities
- Gain Access to Secret IRS Files Kept on You
- Protect your Business . . . and Much More!

The information you receive from this manual makes you a force to reckon with if the IRS begins to make unjustified demands for more of your money. No taxpayer should be without the knowledge provided in this oversized book that is actually nine books in one!

. . .$39.95 plus P&H

How To Get Tax Amnesty

The dischargeability of taxes in bankruptcy was an issue that exploded into the national media through the *Pilla Talks Taxes* Newsletter. The result was an admission by the IRS that taxes were indeed dischargeable in bankruptcy. This led to the installation of tax amnesty programs that have helped millions of people.

These programs are discussed in this book. In all, four tax amnesty programs are available. If you owe taxes you cannot pay, make no mistake. You can be forgiven of all or part of that debt. The Tax Amnesty Book has sold over 180,000 copies. While the programs are still in effect, definite steps have been taken to limit your ability to be forgiven of tax debt.

If you owe tax debt you cannot pay, act now to get Tax Amnesty before your rights are gone. They won't last forever!

. . .$15.95 plus P&H

PILLA TALKS TAXES
A Monthly Newsletter and Consultation Service

Pilla Talks Taxes is a monthly tax exposé. Keeping a constant vigil over lawmakers in Washington, Dan reports the behind-the-scenes truth about pending legislation and changes in tax law. Rarely do we get the whole truth about changes that are supposed to simplify your tax life or lower your taxes. Without *Pilla Talks Taxes* you could find out too late you were sold a bill of goods instead of a bill of rights.

This newsletter is powerful in its effect on lawmakers and the laws they pass. Key members of the media and members of Congress read this newsletter. This provides a national platform on which many obscure bits of tax legislation can be exposed to and discussed by the public.

For example, this newsletter exposed one's ability to get tax amnesty then contributed to the much-publicized discussion over the Taxpayers' Bill of Rights Act. *Pilla Talks Taxes* played a key roll in defeating the first version of the bill, a version proven by Dan Pilla to take away rights rather than provide new ones. Subsequent to its defeat, a new version of the bill was passed--one that actually provided taxpayers with new rights.

As a subscriber to this newsletter, you are also granted special privileges. It has always been the purpose of Dan Pilla and Winning Publications, Inc., to provide citizens with affordable solutions to devastating tax problems. That's why subscribers to PTT get . . .

ONE FREE HOUR OF PERSONAL CONSULTATION

This personal consultation with Dan Pilla makes this newsletter one of the best informational values on the market today.

. . . $127.00

Stairway to Freedom--A Videotape Presentation

For years, author and Tax Litigation Consultant Daniel J. Pilla has conducted this exciting and dynamic seminar for audiences across the nation. Now, this seminar is available on videotape.

The *Stairway to Freedom* Video Seminar is a 90-minute power-packed presentation by the nation's leading IRS expert and proponent of taxpayers' rights. Dan informs and entertains you on topics of importance to each of us--your taxpayers' rights.

In this presentation, you learn:
- Six rights every taxpayer must know
- How to cut your taxes and claim more deductions
- How to audit-proof and penalty-proof your tax return
- Secrets that will keep you out of IRS trouble.

. . . $19.95 plus P&H

Tax Amnesty Forms Kit and Resource Guide

In this kit, find all the forms you need to expedite your claim to tax debt forgiveness. Whether you need to appeal collection actions, stop wage levies, cancel liens or eliminate tax debt altogether, the form you need for the job is in this kit.

Additionally, this kit includes important IRS publications and instructions. Learn how to prepare protests, request release of federal liens, use the Problem Resolution program and much, much more.

Use this kit in conjunction with the book, *How to Get Tax Amnesty*. These two items complement each other perfectly.

. . . $9.95 postpaid

Smart Tax Forms Kit

Find in this kit all the forms you need to put into practice all that you learn in Dan's latest book, *How to Double Your Tax Refund.* This kit includes:

- Exclusive Recordkeeping Techniques
- Reproducible Forms
- Customized Log Sheets

The information in this kit will help you in many important areas:

- Avoid IRS Investigations
- Increase Your Refund
- Keep Financial Records Private
- Prevent Penalty assessments
- Save Money and Time

. . . $6.95 postpaid

Be sure to look for upcoming titles in our Smart Tax series.

- How to Turn Your Hobby Into a Business
- How to Make Your Home a Tax-free Retirement Account
- How to Maximize Hidden Benefits For Charitable Giving

Periodically check our website or call 800-34-NOTAX

If you want to subscribe to *Pilla Talks Taxes* or want to purchase any of our WINNING Publications, call the toll-free number listed below and ask about special subscriber offers or package price opportunities. You can also visit our website for the latest and greatest information.

1-800-34-NOTAX
WINNING Publications, Inc.
2372 Leibel Street
White Bear Lake, MN 55110

www.taxhelponline.com